From
KING'S HEATH
to the Country

including Maypole, Yardley Wood
and Happy Valley

— A view from the past —

Barrie Geens

Barrie Geens

KRM Publishing
Kidderminster Railway Museum
Station Approach
Comberton Hill
Kidderminster
Worcestershire
DY10 1QX

ISBN 0 9534775 6 8

Printed in Great Britain by
Amadeus Press, Cleckheaton

— ACKNOWLEDGEMENTS —

I am grateful for the help that has been given to me in the preparation of this
book by the following people:

Stan and Molly Budd, Birmingham Reference Library, Alan Wycherley,
T.J. Edgington, Mike Rhodes, Kate Keown, Sheila Powell, Ed Sumner,
David and Elsie Lukeman, Barry Dale, Duncan Chew, Peter Topley,
Phil Coutanche, Michael Williams, Roger Carpenter, R.J. Buckley, Mike Trueman,
Dorothy and Bill Newell, David Postle, and to my wife Sue for her patience
and encouragement.

— Contents —

Front Cover: King's Heath High Street

Back Cover: *Top* - Maypole Lane , 1916
Bottom - Refreshment Rooms at Happy Valley just prior to the First World War

Title Page: Tram 363 at the terminus outside the Kings Arms, Alcester Lanes End on 10th September 1949. The driver and conductress wait for time at the Bundy clock before setting off to town via Balsall Heath. A gent, suitably refreshed, waits for the bus to Maypole.

A. N. Glover, courtesy Alan Wycherley

My parents Herbert and Phyllis Geens (née Keeley) at their wedding reception
at Kingsfield on 25th March 1933.

— Introduction —

I was born in King's Heath just prior to the Second World War and lived all my childhood years in Goldsmith Road, memories of which now constantly fill my thoughts. These were the days when motorised vehicles were few and far between and the milkman, baker and coalman all plied their trade with a horse and cart. I have always suffered with 'nostalgia' and have been a collector of images and ephemera for a number of years fuelling my passion. I remember with fondness watching the steam trains pass through King's Heath Station and to this day wish I had owned my own camera to record the images. I expect the railway was in my blood as my father had worked for the London and North Western Railway before becoming a bus driver with the Birmingham City Transport and driving the 18A bus from Yardley Wood Garage.

I attended Wheelers Lane Infant, Junior and Secondary Boys School before spending many happy hours working for Cadbury Brothers at Bournville. My latter years were spent working for the Education Welfare Service where I had the pleasure of working with the schools in the King's Heath area.

My interest in the old days did not wane over the years and for a time I served on the committee of the King's Heath Local History Society before leaving the area in 1993.

I have for a long time wanted to produce a book on the area of King's Heath and to share my collection with others. I have travelled the country to post card fairs searching for the 'rare' King's Heath card, spent many hours at the Birmingham Reference Library searching for photographs, documents and news items. I also had the pleasure of knowing the late Stan Budd who with his wife, Molly was very helpful to me. Stan was a man with great knowledge of the area and his help has proved invaluable in the preparation of this book.

6

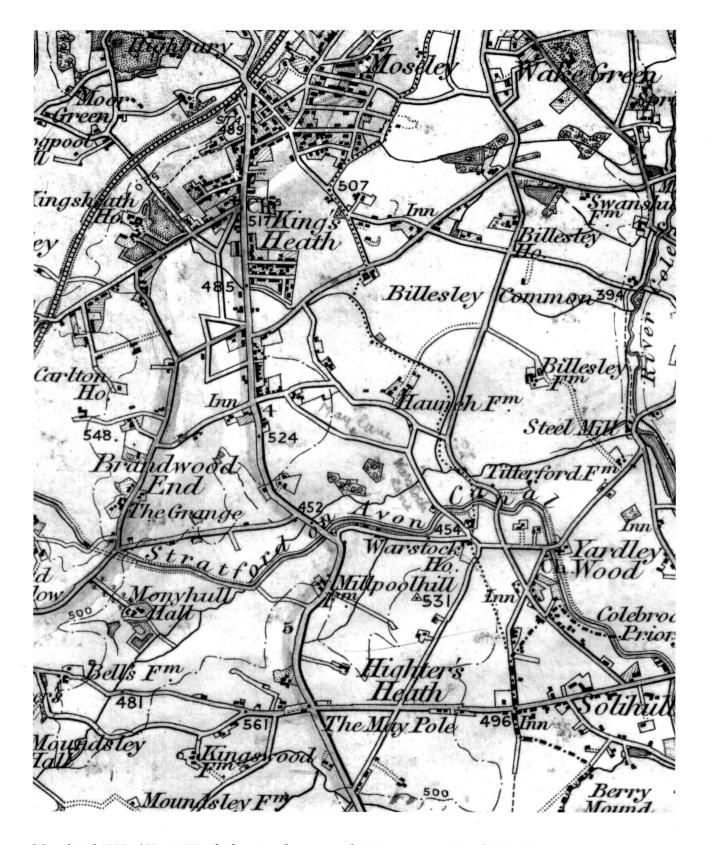

Map dated 1895 of King's Heath showing the geographical area covered by this book. *Crown copyright*

— HISTORY —

King's Heath is now a thriving suburb of Birmingham just four miles south of the City centre. It has not always been in Birmingham, however, as its history goes back to the reign of William the Conqueror (Rex Willielmus). In 1086, the area formed part of the Manor of Bromsgrove which was held by King William in demesne, with eighteen Berewicks: - Muselie (Moseley), Nortune (King's Norton), etc. Earl Edwin held this manor in the time of Edward the Confessor. Hence the district was called King's Heath, as it was within the Royal manor of King's Norton.

The earliest known mention of King's Heath is to be found in a deed in the possession of Mr W. B. Bickley. Written in contracted Latin, and dated 17th August '33, Hen. VIII. (1541). It describes a piece of land as lying near the Heath called "Kingisheithe", in the holding of Bartholomew More. There were further mentions in 1655 and then in 1759, when an improvable Freehold Estate was offered for sale. The property was described as "lying by the side of King's Heath, near Moseley".

In the early 17th century and prior to early development both King's Heath and Moseley were said to be thickly wooded with heavily timbered pastures, cultivated lands with enormous hedges and ditches, rough lanes, heaths and commons with here and there a half timbered homestead.

The attractions for new settlers to the area were clay, which was suitable for brick making, timber and flax, but it was the improvement of the turnpike road which really began to put the area on the map. In 1767 an Act of Parliament was passed for repairing and widening the road from Spernall Ash, through Studley to Digbeth in Birmingham. The new turnpike road as described "would pass through Alcester Lane, Moseley Lane and over Ball's Hall Heath". To

reach Birmingham along this road when it was completed in the early nineteenth century the traveller would have to pay several tolls. It was in the early eighteenth century that the first signs of development began to appear with the building of farms and cottages but it was on completion of the Turnpike Road (Alcester Road) in the early nineteenth century that local development began to increase. Reports from 1855 say that Toll gates were still in existence in three places, one at the corner of Poplar Road, one by the station and another in Valentine Road. These had all disappeared by the late 1870s. It was also during the 1850s that the Baptist Church was without a minister and a local preacher from Silver Street officiated. Opposite the Baptist Church there were just a few houses which were rather small and of unpretentious design. In one of these properties was the village post office and in addition to running this important job, the proprietor also carried on the business of a grocer, milk seller and butcher. King's Heath at this time could not support a doctor with patients having to journey to Bordesley Station to consult one. One of the popular activities for youngsters at this time would be to walk from King's Heath, through the fields to the Lickey Hills. It would certainly be difficult to imagine this happening today!

The rapid growth of the area in the latter part of the nineteenth century can be largely attributed to the arrival of the Birmingham to Gloucester railway line which opened with a station at the Moseley end of the village in 1840. The appeal of living in the area was further enhanced when the steam tram service was extended to King's Heath on February 1st 1887. In 1878 prior to the introduction of the tram service, the houses were mainly those of the working class, with a small number of the middle class and gentry. A number of shops were also evident. Between Moseley and King's Heath the houses were few in number and almost without exception gentlemen's residences. The wages in the district were low, as there were no manufactories or workshops of any importance. Most of the adult male inhabitants were then employed in agriculture, brewing, brick making (the brick yard was at the back of the High Street Council Schools), button making and the manufacture of fire irons, with wages varying from fifteen shillings (75p) to twenty five shillings (£1.25) per week.

In 1885 the footpaths were merely gravel paths with no curbs and from the present police station to the Grange Drive (now Grange Road) was a pleasant green field with a row of beautiful red chestnuts. Opposite where the 'Kingsway' later stood was King's Heath Brewery and along this side of the road there was only one shop which was at the corner of Silver Street, then a cul-de-sac known as 'The Pudding Bag'. No trams ran to King's Heath but there was a horse bus driven from Alcester Lanes End to Moseley Village about three times a day. Only one road led out of the village street, and this was Poplar Road. The village boasted four public houses: 'The Yew Tree' (known as Drinkwater's), 'The George' on what is now The Parade, 'The Cross Guns', and 'The Hare and Hounds'. Before The Parade was built along with the Kingsway, small cottages hugged the roadway all along this stretch of the village.

There are few districts which can compare with King's Heath in the rapidity with which it leaped into favour as a residential resort. In the 1880s it was nothing more than a wayside village with the usual quota of hostelries, and a cluster of time-worn cottages. Wealthy manufacturers had moved from Birmingham to live in the district. Two of these were John Cartland at the Priory and William Hamper at the Grange. In 1895 William Hamper sold the Grange, a late eighteenth century mansion, to the Birmingham Freehold Land Society and in 1898 it was demolished when the building of the present

terraced housing estate around Grange and Station Road began. The area once had a number of large residences housing prominent local people, including the Priory (site now occupied by the King Edwards Camp Hill Schools), home of the Cartlands, Highbury, home of Joseph Chamberlain MP and Uffculme, the Richard Cadbury residence. Hazelwell Hall, which was built on an estate dating back to 1325, was the most important private house until 1800.

All Saints Church is situated at the highest point in King's Heath village at just over 517 ft above sea level. The 'Cross Guns' at Alcester Lanes End is a little higher at 520 ft above sea level. Alcester Lanes End was a popular place as the sender of a post card in 1913 wrote "*Crowds of folk come to Alcester Lane on Saturdays and Sundays and trams follow each other every few minutes loaded with townspeople*".

The road names we know today were somewhat different in the nineteenth century. Woodthorpe Road was called Tom Gough's Lane. Taylor Road was Jack Guest's Lane, Featherstone Road was Featherbed Lane, at the corner of which was Seamore Greaves' Public House. Poplar Road was Adam's Lane and Billesley Lane was Bully Lane. Part of Dads Lane had its name changed to Avenue Road in 1871, after Mr Cartland created his 'avenue' of trees. May Lane was also known as 'Lovers Lane' in which there was not enough room for two carts to pass each other. Vicarage Road was known as Bleak, Black or Blake Lane and ran through green meadows, while other roads running from the main Alcester Road were also buried into rusticity.

In the 1850s Poplar Road, Silver Street and the main road comprised the then King's Heath, with a total population of 700 at the outside. In 1871 this figure was 1,982 and by 1919 the population had increased to over 16,000.

By the start of the 20th century King's Heath had been transformed and by 1911 the Worcestershire village which had formerly been part of the King's Norton Ward was now part of the growing City of Birmingham.

Opposite: 1903 map showing the principal locations illustrated in the book. *Crown copyright*

— KING'S HEATH to THE MAYPOLE —

This row of shops on the Alcester Road South between Drayton Road and Addison Road on 18th April 1962 shows the popular Sadler Bros shop for the avid gardener, the Scotch Wool and Hosiery store, Wrensons the grocers and Harrisons the Opticians. The cars of the day grace the road without fear of any parking restrictions.

Birmingham Reference Library

Opposite: A. J. Carter has a fine array of fruit, fish and poultry on display at his store at the junction of Taylor Road and Alcester Road c 1925. This corner has seen a fruit and veg. salesman here for many years.

Author's collection

Addison Road Junction. On 25th May 1955 work is underway converting the corner residence into commercial premises. The window in Addison Road displays Conservative supporting posters for the forthcoming elections and the latest cars are displayed at Barts.

Birmingham Reference Library

Plenty of cars fill the roads in this 1964 scene taken from Addison Road of the Alcester Road South junction and Arnold Genders garage. The advert for the garage dates back to 22nd January 1937.

photo T. J. Edgington

A 1920s view of Alcester Road looking towards High Street from opposite Mossfield Road. Arnold Genders garage is on the left. (See advert for the garage on page 12)

Author's collection

Tramcar 434 on the 42 route heads away from King's Heath village on 16th January 1949. The photographer's Hillman Minx is prominent as the tram is about to pass Middleton Road. Norman Glover always used to include his car in the picture whenever he could.

A. N. H. Glover, courtesy A. Wycherley

Heathfield Cottage, Alcester Road in the late 1800s. For a number of years until the late 1870s, Mr. Moss Todd was the owner of this cottage, a typical old English home cosily embowered in greenery, and one might say surrounded by the quaintest of trim cut hedges, with the silver hollies over the entrance wicket being trimmed and cut as a lych gate. Mr. Moss Todd was also the owner of the 'King's Arms', Alcester Lanes End, and no doubt the road made near the cottage, Mossfield Road, was named after him. A brother, Grove Todd was the owner of the 'Fighting Cocks' at Moseley. After the demise of the Todd family, William McDonald moved in to Heathfield Cottage and it was his gardener, Isaac Shipton who trimmed the hedge in its picturesque shape as it is shown on photographs at this time. The cottage was not listed in the street directory after 1911 which is when Mossfield Road was constructed. The last occupants of the cottage were then listed as living at number 69, Alcester Road.

courtesy Stan Budd

Opposite top: Alcester Road at the 'Jetty'. This view is looking towards King's Heath Village from Howard Road on 6th January 1926. Howard Road East had yet to be constructed and the path towards Wheelers Lane was known as the 'Jetty' with the land to the side being used as allotments. In July 1934 there was much interest when a huge soil excavator arrived to prepare for the construction of the road much to the disappointment of the allotment holders who had received their notices to quit some months earlier. Traffic lights now operate at this very busy junction.

Birmingham Reference Library

Opposite bottom: A 1970s view of Howard Road East before the demolition of the houses.

Author's collection

The water trough and drinking fountain seen at the junction of Tenbury Road, Featherstone Road and Alcester Road. Previous to this location it was situated in the centre of King's Heath at the junction of Vicarage Road where it was erected in 1897 to commemorate Queen Victoria's Diamond Jubilee. Its current whereabouts, if any are unknown.

Birmingham Reference Library

Tram 405 on the 42 route is seen passing the Municipal Bank on the approach to Alcester Lanes End.

A. N. H. Glover, courtesy A. Wycherley

Saturday October 1st 1949 was the last day of the King's Heath tram routes. A normal service operated on this day as did the additional services for the evening's King's Heath Dog Track meeting. This view shows the line up of trams around six o'clock just to the north of Taylor Road. The dog track which was just beyond the terminus closed in March 1971 and is now a housing estate. *A. N. H. Glover, courtesy A. Wycherley*

This scene outside the King's Arms on 17th September 1949 shows tram 423 at the in-bound terminus stop of the 42 route. The 1938 built Daimler bus, EOG 189, will continue to the terminus at the Maypole.

A.N.H.Glover, courtesy A. Wycherley

The Knob

This page and opposite top: A motor cycle group meet outside the King's Arms, Alcester Lanes End c1939.

Birmingham Reference Library

Tram 407 waits to return to King's Heath and town at the Alcester Lanes End terminus outside the King's Arms.

Author's collection

Tram 447 arrives at the Alcester Lanes End terminus. A truly tranquil scene c1915.

Mike Rhodes collection

The local Garage and Cycle Depot on the corner of Woodthorpe Road and Alcester Road just prior to the First World War. A garage of some description has occupied this corner for many years. This garage appears to also be thriving ironmongers. The message on the postcard of 9th July 1914 says *"Notice in picture. 1) The motor garage at the corner of Woodthorpe Road (the road leading to the cemetery) which used to be a stone masons. 2) The new houses built nearly all the way to Livingstone Road"*.

Author's collection

Howes & Hill's Garage & Cycle Depot at the corner of Woodthorpe Road c1910.   *Author's collection*

Woodthorpe Road looking towards Alcester Lanes End c1930.   *Author's collection*

A nice hooded convertible drops down Mill Pool Hill from Alcester Lanes End c1915. The car, which is approaching a dangerous right hand bend, is not exactly keeping to the left!

Author's collection

Mill Pool Hill Farm and Dairy, proprietor Christopher Hodgetts. In the days before crash helmets, an exhilarating run beckons. This scene c1930s is on Mill Pool Hill opposite Glenavon Road.

courtesy Stan Budd

The Horse Shoe Inn on the Alcester Road at Mill Pool Hill looking north in 1913. This canal side Inn was a popular drinking place during the summer months with fishermen and 'Happy Valley' revellers. Happy Valley could be reached by a short walk along the tow path towards Yardley Wood.   *Author's collection*

Fishermen relaxing by the Stratford on Avon Canal possibly just before the First World War. The message on the back of the card of June 1915 says *"The house beyond the right of the bridge is where I lodge at"*. The Horse Shoe Inn overlooks the scene at the top of the path.   *Author's collection*

Work is starting on the demolition of the old canal bridge carrying the Alcester Road over the Stratford Canal. The Horse Shoe Inn is prominent on the road. 12th April 1938.

Birmingham Reference Library

THE MAYPOLE, HOLLYWOOD.

Published by J. T. Smedley, Hollywood. 2995

The Maypole at the Hollywood boundary in the early years of the 20th century. This scene looking towards Birmingham shows the tall signpost with weather vane and no doubt the scene of many a maypole dance in the nineteenth century.

Author's collection

Morris Imperial bus 509 stands at the Maypole terminus of the City boundary on 16th March 1934. It would take the semi-express 17 service to Erdington.

Birmingham Reference Library

The Maypole Inn, Nr. Birmingham.

A Daimler bus JOJ 53 on the No 50 route arrives at the Maypole terminus in the 1950s. The Maypole Inn which was a land mark for many years is now but a memory. The Maypole Cinema which was also nearby has been replaced by shops in the name of progress.   *Author's collection*

Friday, February 11th, 1938.

MAYPOLE CINEMA

KINGS HEATH.   WARstock 2051

Thursday, February 10th, for three days.

WILL HAY in

OH! MR. PORTER (U)

Sunday, February 13th.

WILLIAM POWELL in **MY MAN GODFREY** (A)
and BUCK JONES in **EMPTY SADDLES** (U).

Monday, February 14th, for three days.

FRANCHOT TONE, MAUREEN O'SULLIVAN, AND VIRGINIA BRUCE in

BETWEEN TWO WOMEN (A)

and full supporting programme.

Matinees Mon., Wed., Thurs.   Popular   Prices   Latest   Deaf   Aid   Equipment
FREE   CAR   PARK   -   CYCLE   ACCOMMODATION

The Maypole Cinema opened on Sunday 1st August 1937 with the film "Keep your seats Please", with George Formby. It was two years previous to this on 19th July 1935 that the King's Heath Observer reported 'Warstock Cinema Application Granted. The Public Entertainment's Committee of the Birmingham Justices on Monday, granted a cinema licence for £20,000 premises to be erected at Alcester Road, Maypole (South Warstock). The applicant was Mr. Ernest A. Turner, of Solihull'. The cinema closed on 26th January 1961 and was demolished to make way for a modern shopping complex.

Maypole Lane Dairyman in 1916.

Author's collection

Two Leyland PD2s wait at the Maypole terminus on 29th August 1949. HOV 657 is on route 35 to Station Street and Paradise Street while HOV 691 waits to return to Moseley Village.

T. J. Edgington

The current Birmingham boundary is at the Maypole where Druids Lane and Maypole Lane meet at the Alcester Road. A scattering of dairy farms pre-dated the current high rise flats and suburban houses. Charles Hodges is seen with his fine delivery hand cart. c1912.

Author's collection

A lady poses by a tree in this very rural scene of King's Heath in June 1893.

Author's collection

Grange Road looking towards the York Road Junction and High Street in the early 1900s. *Author's collection*

—Suburbia & Side Streets—

The comparatively new houses shown opposite were built as a result of the sale of the Grange Estate in 1895 for housing development and was a huge milestone in the development of King's Heath. There were few districts which could compare with King's Heath in the rapidity with which it leaped into favour as a residential resort. In the 1890s it was counted in the local geography as nothing more than a wayside village, with the usual quota of hostelries, and a cluster of time-worn cottages. Within five years however, it was intersected with the lines of the Birmingham Central Tramways Company and with handsome shops, comparable with the like of any to be seen in any other suburb. Away from the main road, lying back in sylvan shrubberies, were well-appointed and elegantly-built modern villas, little Paradises to the careworn city man. The hand of improvement was everywhere; the imposing Institute, and even the extensive and expansive Police Station and Police Court, testified to the growing importance of the suburb. During the summer of 1895 the locality was destined to undergo a development which would eclipse in extent all previous enterprises. The Grange Estate which was so long associated with King's Heath was to be transformed into bricks and mortar through the agency of the Birmingham Freehold Land Society. The expansive stretch of land was surrounded by and overlooked the retreats of Highbury, Uffculme, and the Priory, while across the picturesque panorama of intervening country a view of the Lickey Hills could be obtained.

The Grange was a large mansion built towards the end of the 18th century and the estate covered about 350 acres, with the main access being via a carriage drive from the Turnpike Road.

The house was demolished in 1895, the estate levelled and the gravelly subsoil removed to be used in the foundations of the planned roadways. Existing trees were left where practicable, but those fronting the main road were felled and an iron fence was substituted.

About one thousand building plots were planned with the price per square yard for these plots varying between 1/6d and 12/6d, depending on their position. The most expensive were those for shops on the main road.

The cost of these houses would vary from about £250 to £300 per pair with a rental of between 5/- and 6/6 per week

The most expensive group would be those which fronted onto the railway and overlooked the residences of Mr. Cadbury and Mr. Chamberlain. These would cost about £450 per pair, with a rental close to 10/- per week. No back houses were permitted at all, neither were public houses.

2,400 applications were received for the first 449 lots of building land on offer, which suggests that the King's Heath of 1895 was a desirable area in which to reside. The ballot and formal allocation of plots took place on 7th November 1895. Many of the successful applicants took immediate possession and, where possible, commenced their building forthwith. Some applicants took a long time to start their building in as much as some building operations were still in progress at the time when Birmingham Corporation took over the district in 1911.

An early view of Featherstone Road at the junction with Hazelhurst and Livingstone Roads. *Author's collection*

The neatly cut lawn is a feature in this 1907 post card view of a back garden in Featherstone Road. In the mid to late nineteenth century the road was known as Featherbed Lane due it is said to the number of tramps who slept under the hedges there after their day's journey.

Author's collection

Opposite top: Children pose for the camera in Abbots Road at the junction with Hazelhurst Road c1917. *Author's collection*

Opposite bottom: 1950-built Leyland PS2 single decker leaves Abbots Road King's Heath for Northfield in the 1960s. *Robert F. Mack*

A 1936 view of Harry and Charlotte Sharp standing outside 'The Cottage' which was known as Sharps' Pop Shop. It stood at the bottom of Brandwood Road close to the Stratford on Avon canal and by the side of the cottage greenhouse was a small path which led to the tow path. A resident close to the Broad Lane tunnel mouth recalled the times in their school holidays when the bargees used to unhitch the horses at the tunnel entrance at the bottom of their garden, and walk them across the corner of Broad Lane and Monyhull Hall Road to meet the barge which had been 'legged' through the tunnel to continue its journey. When at home in the school holidays they could hear the jingling of the harnesses, and would rush up the lane on their bikes to see the horses walked up the tow path track and be re-hitched across the road. *courtesy Stan Budd*

Opposite top: An early view of Hazelhurst Road, not yet with a tarmac surface, looking towards Howard Road before the extension to Abbots Road was cut.

Author's collection

Opposite bottom: The Siviter children and maid pose c1902 at 214, Alcester Road (South) on the corner of Livingstone Road. Mr Siviter, who had recently built the house, stands in the garden. *courtesy Sheila Powell*

Brandwood Road looking like a leafy country lane. A far cry from today's busy scene. *Author's collection*

Brandwood Road looking north c1930. *Mike Rhodes collection*

Silver Street on a cold winter's day in the 1960s. Tommy Godwin's was the top cycling shop in King's Heath for many years. A 1948 Olympic Cyclist, Tommy had a great wealth of experience to call on which drew enthusiasts of the sport in from a wide area. An earlier cycle shop in Silver Street was Hughes Cycles, whose advert from 27th May 1938 appears below.

courtesy Stan Budd

CYCLE to HEALTH

Ride the *Real* QUALITY Bicycle B.S.A

It means so much more if you ride a B.S.A.—so much more in comfort and easy-running, because every single feature from end to end of a B.S.A. Bicycle is a Quality feature. You can't go wrong if you choose a B.S.A.

From **£5.10s.** or 2/6 weekly

HUGHES & SON, SILVER STREET, KINGS HEATH

Phone HIGHbury 2592.

An early view of Station Road looking towards the High Street. *courtesy Mike Rhodes*

An early postcard view of Pineapple Road with the new Hazelwell Station, built less than seven years earlier, on the sky line in the centre distance at the top of Cartland Road. The message on the card of 31st August 1908 says *"Such a day! Sheets of rain and half a gale since midday. Hope you have not got the same"*. The card was addressed to Mrs. Rupert Smith at "Brandwood" Aberdovey. How ever did it get delivered without a street name and a post code?!

Author's collection

An early post card view dated 11th September 1909 of 'Pineapple Bridge', Vicarage Road looking towards King's Heath before any modern housing development had started. Pineapple Farm is on the right. Between the years 1777 and 1787, Pineapple Farm was in the occupation of Mr Joseph Grove and consisted of a farm house, outhouses, garden and about 31 acres of arable and meadow land.

Author's collection

The old Pineapple road bridge looking towards Stirchley on 15th August 1924.

Birmingham Reference Library

The old Pineapple road bridge looking towards King's Heath on 15th August 1924.

Birmingham Reference Library

The new Pineapple road bridge over the railway on 7th October 1930.

Birmingham Reference Library

Dads Lane Farm on 14th December 1925 prior to demolition in 1926. The farm was bought for housing development from J. Austen Chamberlain. This view is looking towards Shutlock Lane which can be seen in the right distance.   *Birmingham Reference Library*

The old Dads Lane railway bridge on 25th February 1931 looking towards Avenue Road *(above)* and from Avenue Road *(below)*.   *Birmingham Reference Library*

The old barns in Dads Lane on 27th January 1926.

Birmingham Reference Library

A Victorian view of Vicarage Road Post Office. No. 281, 'North View', near to the junction with Kings Road advertises R.Whites Lemonade, Fry's Cocoa and Chocolate and Woodbine Cigarettes. *Author's collection*

In the early 1850s it is said that there was no post office in the King's Heath. If you wanted a letter you had to fetch it from Moseley. If the postman brought it up he would charge 2d.

By 1854 a primitive postal service operated in King's Heath as letters arrived from Birmingham by foot post at 8am and were dispatched at 6pm.

In 1894 there appeared to be a better delivery service than the standard we are used to today. A letter posted in town by 4.30.a.m. would be delivered in King's Heath at 7.30 a.m. the same day!

In September 1896 the Moseley Society Journal reported "*A petition is being numerously signed praying the postal authorities to extend the facilities of delivery of letters in the King's Heath district. That at present there is no Sunday delivery, and those expecting letters have to send to the local post office for them at an early hour. That this state of affairs ought not, and cannot, remain much longer in so important and growing a district.*"

Success was noted in the August 1897 issue of the Moseley Soc. Journal when it was reported. "*Thanks to the efforts of Mr. John Findon, of Tudor House, King's Heath, the whole of the district now enjoys a Sunday postal delivery. Hitherto through the inscrutable decrees of the powers of the post office only the residents on the main road enjoyed the boon of a Sabbath delivery of letters, the remainder having to either send to the local office before ten in the morning, or wait till the following Monday morning. Such a state of affairs would not be tolerated in a country village, and why the King's Heath people in a matter so closely touching their interest should have tolerated it so long is another mystery. However, Mr. Findon has agitated, canvassed for a memorial, roused the local governing bodies, engaged the interest and influence of Mr. Austen Chamberlain, M.P., and after a twelve month wait the consummation has arrived.*"

I don't think the same pressure today would gain a similar result!

Vicarage Road from Avenue Road on 19th April 1923. King's Heath Park is on the right and as the houses had not yet been built in Vicarage Road a glimpse of Colmore Road Council School can be seen to the left.

Birmingham Reference Library

Vicarage Road near to the junction of Kings Road, c1930. The big house on the left used to be a nursing home and is where my sister and I were born.

Author's collection

Vicarage Road looking towards the village from Abbots Road, c1910.   *Author's collection*

A busy scene on Vicarage Road as a 1964 built Daimler bus is seen passing Kings Road on its Outer Circle journey to the Kings Head.   *Alan B. Cross*

Reeves Road in the late 1920s. *Author's collection*

A 1921 view of Valentine Road. Three carefree lady cyclists head down the hill towards the High Street.

Author's collection

Addison Road c1912 looking towards High Street with 'Pretoria Grocery Stores' on the corner of Goldsmith Road being the focal point.
Author's collection

Hedge cutting is in progress in this early scene in Springfield Road. The view is looking north from the junction of Institute Road and Billesley Lane.
courtesy Mike Rhodes

A horse awaits its next call of duty in this peaceful scene of Poplar Road.

Author's collection

The newsagents and stationers shop is prominent in this postcard view of Poplar Road. Newspaper boards occupy the pavement including an advertisement for London. There also seems to be a plentiful supply of postcards in the window.

Author's collection

Haunch Lane in 1935, looking from Yardley Wood Road or the 'Valley' as it was known. The number 18A bus terminus shelter and the Tudor Cinema are prominent to the right and the car park to the Valley Public House is to the left of the picture. *Birmingham Reference Library*

Haunch Lane looking towards Wheelers Lane in 1932. *Birmingham Reference Library*

Drayton Road looking towards Goldsmith Road. The cyclist has just avoided the photographer and is now negotiating a recent deposit of garden fertiliser c1915. *Author's collection*

A 1920s view of Cambridge Road, looking towards the church and the village. *Author's collection*

Portman Road houses under construction in April 1935. Number 22, seen here, was being purchased by the Sumner family for £600. *Ed Sumner*

A wintry 1941 World War 2 bomb damage scene in Wheelers Lane. *Birmingham Reference Library*

Members of the Keeley family outside 54, Coldbath Road about 1908 with my grandmother and eldest aunts and uncles. *Author's collection*

Opposite top: Hadley's Farm at the corner of Wheelers Lane during the making of Hollybank Road in 1932. The dairy farm was the main milk supplier for the area.

Birmingham Reference Library

Opposite bottom: A 1928 postcard view of Institute Road with children posing for the camera near the junction with Goldsmith Road. *Author's collection*

Celebration party for the children of Coldbath Road, May 1937.   *Author's collection*

George VI Coronation Day celebrations May 1937

Keeley, Geens and Dymond family members outside 9, Coldbath Road at the time of the coronation celebrations.

Author's collection

Right and below: Coronation Day party in Milford Place off High Street in May 1937.

Dorothy Newell collection

Children pose in this early High Street scene near to Poplar Road. The newsagents on the left of the picture has occupied this site for many years. In my younger years it was Darlastons and was the last shop before the Kingsway Picture House. The advert below dates from 27.10.49.   *Author's collection*

Announcing that :
E. A. DARLASTON
75 HIGH STREET KINGS HEATH   HIG. 2015
HAS BEEN APPOINTED BOOKING AGENT FOR

— HIGH STREET —

Chapman and Sanders shop on the High Street opposite Institute Road. It was always a mouth-watering experience looking through the window as a young boy as on display were the latest Dinky toys, Hornby Dublo trains and Meccano sets. The history of the ownership was that Jessie Chapman and Miss Sanders were the original owners of the shop. Jessie Chapman was engaged to a Harry Deakin but Harry's work took him to Manitoba for several years. When he returned about 1910 he married Jessie and had a house built, No. 2 Hazelhurst Road for £320 by Buggins, a local builder. The site was chosen because it was within walking distance from the shop. Eventually they bought out Miss Sanders share but kept the original name of 'Chapman and Sanders'. Jessie continued to work in the shop until she was in her eighties and then it was managed by her niece Gwen Fowler and a close friend Edna Jowett.

courtesy Stan Budd

Tascos originally opened a shop in King's Heath during 1902 when Branch 4 grocery opened at 44, Poplar Road, transferring in 1904 to Heathfield Road. It was between 1912 and 1917 that a drapery, clothing and boot, and a bread shop opened here. In 1917, a retail coal-yard was acquired at King's Heath Station and during the 1940s this was one of five main depots situated at railway stations, the others being at Lifford, Northfield, Selly Oak and Bromsgrove. In 1930, Branch 24, grocery and allied departments opened in High Street, followed in 1935 by Branch 24, also in High Street, which opened for chemistry. In 1937 this branch was considerably extended and modernised and opened for ladies hairdressing over the chemistry shop. Seeking to extend its activities, Tascos purchased a number of businesses after the end of the war in 1945, namely in Broad Lane (Branch 37) and Vicarage Road (Branch 35). In addition to the purchasing of these businesses the society leased a pre-fabricated building in Winterbourne Crescent, Druid's Lane, which was opened as the society's first self-service shop. The idea of self-service, which came to Britain from America, was intended not only to economise in labour, but also to effect saving in the time entailed in shopping by the customer. The co-operative movement was the first one in the midlands to be fitted specially as a self-service shop. A butchery branch also opened in Winterbourne Crescent.

There were also branches at Alcester Lanes End (Branch 13), which was one of three confectionery branches, and in School Road, Yardley Wood (Branch 17) which opened in 1922. In 1926, Branch 18 in Yardley Wood Road, Billesley, opened for butchery and confectionery.

In 1931, Branch 25, in Prince of Wales Lane, Warstock, opened for grocery and butchery. In 1937, Branch 32, at Maypole also opened for grocery and butchery.

Opposite and this page: Tascos branch 24, in the small shop next to the Co-op dry goods shop on the High Street. Situated next to the Baptist Church, it was converted to 'self service' around 1948 and these three photographs were taken soon after conversion. In the mid 1950s the grocery dept. moved down the High Street and the dry goods dept. expanded into what was the grocery area. The dry goods store (or 'Emporium') stayed open until the mid 1980s. 'In Shops' occupied the premises in recent years.

photograph above courtesy Barry Dale, opposite and below Author's collection

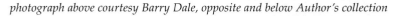

Blackwell's Fish and Poultry shop at number 112A High Street c1930s. The shop was situated between Silver Street and York Road.

courtesy Peter Blackwell

Opposite top: The old cottages on the site now occupied by Somerfields. Charles Elton established the butcher's business in 1770 and was also the sub-postmaster next door. The butchers shop in this view, c1910 was owned by William Bluck. *courtesy Stan Budd*

Advert for the Milk Bar (*see opposite*) dated 1952

Griffith's fishmongers and poultry shop at 112A High Street was in business in the 1920s and was later taken over by Blackwell's.

courtesy Peter Blackwell

The old row of shops where the modern Safeway, (now Somerfields) was built. Kings the Jewellers, Simpson's the Butchers and Babyland ply their trade on 16th June 1954. Two shops beyond the gap at No. 111 High Street was the 'Milk Bar' which plied its trade in the 1940s and 1950s.   *Birmingham Reference Library*

Bailey's Confectioners Shop at 151, High Street c1925. This was next to King's Heath School or close to where McDonalds now stands. The shop specialised in making cakes and bread on the premises. A sign in the shop window advertises 'Yestamin Bread, the whole loaf with health promoting Vitamin B'. *courtesy Stan Budd*

G. R. Bailey, horse-drawn bakers and confectioners delivery cart in Waterloo Road. *courtesy Stan Budd*

Lashfords Butchers was part of the King's Heath scene for many years. It was first listed in the Kellys Directory of 1912, having taken over the business from Mrs Florence Rose. In this early scene the butchers pose for the camera but it could be sad times as a horse-drawn hearse stands in Poplar Road. The last listing for the business was in the 1971-2 directory.

courtesy Stan Budd

Cattle await their fate in the yard at the rear of Lashfords butchers shop in Poplar Road.

courtesy Stan Budd

This 1926 view of High Street taken from York Road shows the entrance to the Ideal Picture House just beyond the Hare and Hounds.

Author's collection

The Ideal Picture House opened its doors for the first time on 5th February 1913.

In March 1914 a local news paper editorial stated…*"The "Ideal" Picture House, in High Street, King's Heath, is, without doubt, suitably named, both building and entertainments being of a very high order, and the immense audiences which repeatedly fill the house prove it to be a popular place for a few hours' real fun and enjoyment. A well-lighted entrance leads into a comfortable crush hall capable of providing waiting room from the bad weather for some 500 persons. Passing from here into the hall itself, the eye at once meets a spacious well-furnished hall to accommodate 550 persons seated, with a wide promenade running along the rear of the hall. A good view of the pictures is obtainable from all parts. Heating and ventilating arrangements are carried out to a nicety. There are four wide exits to the hall, two large electric fans carry all foul air through the roof, and in the operator's room safety patent iron shutters are placed inside and outside the walls, affording a sure protection to the public in case* of fire. If necessary, the whole building can be completely emptied in under one minute's time. Patrons of the "Ideal" Picture House are assured of seeing exhibited first-class pictures, which are shown on a silvered screen, an arrangement which adds to their brilliancy".

The September 1914 issue of the Birmingham Moseley & King's Heath Society Journal editorial reported *"In spite of the unsettled condition of things generally, owing to the War, the attendances at the "Ideal" Picture House, in High Street, King's Heath, so far have shown no signs of becoming less. While giving our readers some idea of the films which will be exhibited during this month, we should like to point out that the arrangements may here and there be modified during the next few weeks, owing to matters indirectly connected with the War, and therefore beyond the control of the management. A special feature at each entertainment at the "Ideal" house will be an exhibition of War Pictures taken at the front these will be kept quite up-to-date and will prove interesting and instructive as to what is going on at the seat of fighting".*

The September 1916 Journal editorial says *"Early in October the energetic manager of the "Ideal" (Mr. Ernest Ellerslie) has arranged for the production of the official War film, "the Battle of the Somme," which will be shown in five parts. Watch the poster announcements and book early,* *for we prophesy the accommodation at the Ideal house will on this occasion be taxed to the uttermost"*.

The Ideal competed with the newly opened Kingsway for a while before closing in April 1932.

F. W. Barr, Pork Butcher at 125 High Street c1910. Each batch of carcases is described with a 'Bread & Fed' notice, e.g. 'Bred & Fed by J. Bartlett Esq. Pear Tree Farm, Yardley Wood. Age 9 months'. Not too many concerns about food hygiene in those days! *John Bick collection*

The row of shops by Poplar Road looking towards town in 1912.   *Author's collection*

Lukemans Forge and Veterinary Surgeon at what is now the bottom end of the Parade. Charles Lukeman had his business here from the late 1880s until 1905. His sign read *"Horses carefully shod and jobbing work attended to"*. The forge then transferred to new premises in Grange Road and then later to York Road. *courtesy David Lukeman*

A 1930s view of the Parade and Kingsway Picture House.

Author's collection

The Kingsway Picture House was a focal point in the village for many years and the following was written at the time of its opening on Monday, March 2nd, 1925.

"In the days of old this was Royal land, truly the King's heath and the King's own way, for Charles the First came here. It is a far cry from those days to 1925. King's Heath is a heath no longer. Houses have grown up, the village has grown and now it is one of the finest suburbs of England's second city.

In recent years the district has grown rapidly, and with the growth came the need for high-class amusement tastefully presented.

In 1913 a scheme was launched for the erection of a Super Cinema – troublesome times intervened, and not till ten years later could any material progress be made.

Now, at last, has risen the Kingsway Cinema, noble, beautiful, efficient, luxurious and comfortable. No longer need the residents of King's Heath and Moseley endure the weariness of trams to town for their entertainment – and the more weary journey home. Here, in their midst, is the

Kingsway, possessed of a delightful Orchestra, showing every good picture that is issued, and more comfortable than the cinemas in the centre of the city.

In the Entrance Hall and Auditorium are large paintings illustrating the times of King Charles, taken from the originals by Gibbs of Stratford-on-Avon.

The predominant colour of the interior is Orange blended with a delicate Green in wall decoration and reflected in upholstery and carpets, while soft lights of beautiful colours suffuse the building".

The Grand Opening Night film was 'Down to the sea in ships' with the celebrated baritone, Mr Fred Bennett singing to the picture. The Kingsway Symphony Orchestra was under the direction of Mr. Shirley North.

On March 5th 1937 the Kingsway Cinema re-opened after undergoing extensive alterations and improvements. The extensions allowed for the seating of 200 or more extra patrons. The King's Heath Observer reported *"There is no doubt that the residents in this district will be pleased at the re-opening of their favourite Cinema. An excellent programme has been arranged for Sunday, and for the following six days".*

My childhood memory of the 1940s and 50s was attending the Children's Club at 10 o'clock on Saturday mornings for the princely sum of 6d. watching cartoons and cowboy films with a sometimes rowdy audience.

The Kingsway closed its doors on 3rd May 1980 and became a bingo hall.

Old cottages in High Street c1890 in the area where the Parade was later built.

Birmingham Reference Library

The old cottages in lower High Street by Grange Road before the Parade and Kingsway were built.

courtesy Stephen Penker

The little row of shops opposite Station Road with the familiar architecture still evident today. Greens, seed and corn merchants operated here until the 1930s. Proffitt and Westwood then occupied the site for many years.

Author's collection

High Street at the Station Road junction on 10th March 1954. Two nice vintage cars make the scene.

Birmingham Reference Library

A lovely scene by Institute Road. A tram heads to town, a motor cycle combination heads out and a policeman watches the children as they leave King's Heath School. *Author's collection*

The row of shops opposite Institute Road featuring 'Avery' Ironmongers to 'Chapman and Sanders', c1920.

Author's collection

A tram heads out of High Street towards Alcester Lanes End by Kingsfield Road. The sender of the postcard in 1914 wrote *"The square block of shops is just where the entrance to Mr Buller's used to be"*. (*Mr Buller was a prominent local resident, J.P. and City solicitor*) *"The road is a cul de sac at present but will be continued to the right of Mr Buller's into a new road at the back (Mayfield Road) which is rather a crooked road starting from the main road to the right of the cottage with the hedges cut beehive fashion"*. Mayfield Road and its extension never came to fruition and the road was called Kingsfield Road after Kingsfield House in the nearby grounds. *Author's collection*

Tram 415 on the 40 route is just about to cross back over on 9th July 1949 after terminating at King's Heath.

T. J. Edgington

68

Below: A policeman admires his patch and a lad washes his hands in the water trough by All Saints Church c1910.

Author's collection

Above: The row of shops c1910 at the corner of Station Road. The new police courts and administration buildings were planned to be built on the corner of Station Road and High Street but these plans were changed and the land was sold at public auction on 21st March 1901. The library seen here, which was built in 1905, stands alone next to the police station stables. The Library opened in 1906 and cost £3,000 to build, the money being generously donated by the Carnegie Foundation. The first Librarian was William Skelton and was under the control of the District Council.

Author's collection

A peaceful scene of Vicarage and All Saints Roads from the High Street in 1908.

Author's collection

8087. High Street, Kings Heath. H.M&S.L.

Coopers Greengrocers shop opposite All Saint's Church was one of the fixtures and fittings of High Street for many years. The shop first appeared in the 1905 street directory and this view is c1912. I personally remember the shop being very popular in the 1950s but it finally closed around 1960. It was one of the few shops that displayed its goods well onto the pavement.   *Author's collection*

A peaceful traffic free scene at the Vicarage Road junction in 1932. Public toilets are at this time still underground.

Birmingham Reference Library

Four horse drawn cabs and carts grace this High Street scene whilst two trams glide to and from town.

courtesy Stephen Penker

Foden, the King's Heath Pharmacy shop at number 50 High Street, recent home of 'Bike Pro' cycle shop.

courtesy Stephen Penker

F. W. Woolworth's store at the corner of Institute Road in 1934. On the site of the former Institute, the store has been on this site for a number of years and is adjoined at this time by Timpson's Shoe shop.

Birmingham Reference Library

This house on the corner of High Street and York Road was next to the Hare and Hounds public house. The buildings were constructed between 1824 and 1828 by Aaron Payton and in a deed dated 1843 this house was said to be used as a police station. The next mention in 1896 describes it as in the occupation of George Blaydon, dairyman. A nice selection of bicycles are parked outside in this view c. 1895.

courtesy Stan Budd

M.R.—BIRMINGHAM to KING'S HEATH.—Via Camp Hill

	A.M	A.M	A.M	A.M	A.M	N'N.	P.M	P.M	P.M	P.M	P.M	P.M	P.M	P.M	P.M	P.M	P.M
Birmingham..dep	6 30	8 5	8 37	9 40	1055	12 0	1248	1 *0	1b10	1*15	1b20	1b40	2b10	2 35	3 50	4 30	5 5
Camp Hill	6 40	8 13	8 46	9 48	11 3	12 8	1258	1 8	1 18	1 23	1 28	1 48	2 18	2 43	3 58	4 39	5 13
Brighton Road	..	8 18	8 51	9 52	11 6	1211	1 0	1 11	1 21	1 26	1 31	1 52	2 21	2 46	4 1	4 42	5 17
Moseley	6 50	8 21	8 54	9 55	11 9	1214	1 3	1 14	1 24	1 29	1 34	1 54	2 24	2 49	4 4	4 45	5 20
King's Heath...arr	6 53	8 26	8 58	9 58	1112	1217	1 6	1 17	1 27	1 33	1 38	1 57	2 27	2 52	4 7	4 48	5 23

Birmingham to King's Heath—continued.   SUNDAYS.

	P.M	P.M	P.M	P.M	P.M	P.M	P.M	P.M	P.M	P.M	P.M	P.M	P.M	A.M	P.M	P.M	P.M
Birmingham..dep	5 22	6 *0	6 15	6 40	7 8	7 35	8 15	9 5	9 40	1015	1050	11b7	1117	8 20	1255	4 30	8 30
Camp Hill	5 30	6 8	6 23	6 48	7 16	7 43	8 23	9 13	9 48	1023	1058	1115	1123	8 28	1 3	4 38	8 38
Brighton Road	5 34	6 11	6 27	6 51	7 20	7 47	8 26	9 16	9 51	1026	11 2	1119	1127	8 32	1 6	4 42	8 41
Moseley	5 37	6 14	6 30	6 55	7 24	7 50	8 30	9 19	9 54	1029	11 5	1122	1130	8 35	1 9	4 45	8 44
King's Heath...arr	5 40	6 18	6 33	6 59	7 28	7 53	8 33	9 22	9 58	1032	11 8	1125	1133	8 38	1 12	4 48	8 47

M.R.—KING'S HEATH to BIRMINGHAM.—Via Camp Hill

	A.M	A.M	A.M	A.M	A.M	A.M	A.M	A.M	A.M	A.M	A.M	A.M	P.M	P.M	P.M	P.M	P.M
King's Heath..dep	6 50	7 17	7 53	8 19	8 30	8 39	9 0	9 21	9 34	1025	1110	1215	1 10	1 39	1 54	2 5	2 25
Moseley	6 53	7 20	7 56	8 22	8 32	8 42	9 3	9 24	9 37	1028	1113	1218	1 13	1 42	1 59	2 9	2 29
Brighton Road	6 56	7 23	7 59	8 25	8 35	8 45	9 6	9 28	9 40	1031	1116	1221	1 16	1 45	2 2	2 12	2 32
Camp Hill	7 1	7 26	8 4	8 31	8 41	8 51	9 11	9 33	9 44	1036	1119	1226	1 22	1 50	2 6	2 17	2 36
Birmingham..arr	7 10	7 35	8 12	8 40	8 50	9 0	9 20	9 42	9 53	1045	1128	1235	1 30	2 0	2 15	2 25	2 45

King's Heath to Birmingham—continued.   SUNDAYS.

	P.M	P.M	P.M	P.M	P.M	P.M	P.M	P.M	P.M	P.M	P.M	P.M	P.M	A.M	P.M	P.M	P.M
King's Heath..dep	2 35	3 43	4 51	5 30	6 7	6 50	7*17	7 29	8 25	9 24	..	1010	..	9 59	5 50	9 9	9 41
Moseley	2 38	3 46	4 54	5 33	6 10	6 53	7 20	7 32	8 28	9 27	..	1012	..	10 2	5 53	9 12	9 45
Brighton Road	2 41	3 49	4 57	5 36	6 13	6 56	7 23	7 35	8 31	9 30	..	1015	..	10 5	5 56	9 15	9 48
Camp Hill	2 46	3 54	5 0	5 42	6 19	7 3	7 28	7 41	8 35	9 36	..	1021	..	1010	6 0	9 21	9 54
Birmingham..arr	2 54	4 2	5 10	5 52	6 28	7 14	7 37	7 50	8 44	9 45	..	1030	..	1020	6 9	9 30	10 5

* Saturdays excepted.   b Runs on Saturdays only.

Fares from Birmingham to the undermentioned Stations.
No reduction in return tickets.

	1st class	3rd class			1st class	3rd class
Camp Hill ...	2½d.	1½d.	Moseley ...		4d.	2½d.
Brighton Road	3d.	2d.	King's Heath	...	5d.	3d.

LONDON: 13, St. Stephen's Square, Bayswater, W.

BOARD AND RESIDENCE

From One-and-Half Guineas per week. Easy access to City and West End, close to Kensington Gardens and Westbourne Grove.

THE MISSES MACKAY.

— RAILWAY —

In 1835 there were two proposed routes between Hazelwell and Camp Hill, one through King's Heath & Moseley and one by-passing both. There were strong objections, particularly to the by-pass route and in December of this year a number of meetings took place chaired by the surveyor, Captain Moorsome. The main objector, Mr James Taylor and other local persons interested in the routes held a meeting at the 'Fighting Cocks' public house at Moseley, resulting in a letter to the railway company expressing Mr Taylor's determination to oppose both lines near Moseley. The railway committee replied to Mr Taylor saying they would adhere to their former intention as expressed to him of abandoning unconditionally the line between Moseley Hall and Moor Green. Thankfully the resolution was accepted

A train departs from King's Heath towards Moseley in 1912.

Author's collection

Opposite: A local train timetable from the Moseley and King's Heath Journal dated September 1901.

Birmingham Reference Library

and the Birmingham and Gloucester Railway was finally authorised.

In March 1837 the first contracts were advertised including one of the Birmingham Committee's heaviest between Camp Hill and Moseley. The section from Moseley to Breedon's Cross was estimated by the engineer to cost £21,000 but was tendered for at £25,000.

On 24th April 1838 reference was made to the building of the road over rail bridge by the proposed station. The engineer presented a tender from John Beaty for building a skew bridge @ 8/6 per cubic yard for brickwork exclusive of bricks and 3/- per cubic foot for stone. The bridge was named 'Queens Bridge' after Queen Victoria's succession to the throne in 1837.

The railway, when formed, cut through a portion of the Henbury estate which was owned by Mr. Charles Ratheram until his death on 17th July 1845. The property was then sold to Mr. R. Cadbury, and afterwards added to the grounds of his newly erected mansion, named Uffculme. The Henburys was then pulled down.

At this time the road known as Welch's Hill was diverted, so as to take a straight course over the newly erected railway bridge (the Queen's Bridge). The turnpike road, previous to this diversion, took a circuitous course, and passed by the old house standing close to King's Heath railway station, and up the roadway leading thereto. In May 1933 an old resident of King's Heath informed the local paper of this fact and that the Station Master's house was formerly the village inn known as the 'Fox & Dogs'.

In 1867 a new station north of Moseley tunnel was built at a cost of £978 and Moseley old station at King's Heath was rebuilt costing £987. The plan already approved for King's Norton station was adopted for the rebuilding of Moseley old station, which was thereafter called King's Heath, and the new station north of Moseley tunnel became Moseley station. The new station at Moseley opened on 1st November 1867.

A report in Everson's Directory of 1896 reported that on the railway line between King's Heath and Moseley stations could be seen one of the best sections of drift to be found in the neighbourhood of Birmingham. In this drift, it is stated, so far as can be ascertained, there is no evidence of ice action; and it is suggested that the beds in King's Heath are merely remnants of an old sea beach that existed once upon a time.

On March 25th 1909 an Arts and Crafts and Loan Exhibition was held in the Cambridge Road Wesleyan Church Schools. Crowds of visitors patronised the exhibition and much interest was shown in the numerous exhibits. One "side show," consisting of a large model of King's Heath Railway Station, made by Mr. Walter C. Russell of Addison Road, complete with miniature rails, and a mechanical train in motion, was largely patronised, and the model admired by all who saw it. I wonder if this model still exists in any form?

A blotting pad used by T. A. Eaves Coal Merchants. Thomas Arthur Eaves was one of the longest serving coal merchants at King's Heath, trading there from 1879 to 1954.

courtesy Stan Budd

The station staff pose for the photographer outside the Station Master's Office on the Down platform c1912. John Brayne, centre front, was Station Master from 1904 until his death in 1930. Note the station name on the seat back and the superb Cape Hill Brewery poster on the wall behind. *courtesy Michael Williams*

This view of the main entrance to the station, yard and coal offices from the High Street was taken on 22nd October 1962. The trams had long since been replaced by buses. The array of cars, advertising hoardings and the British Railways sign on the corner are all evocative of the period.

Birmingham Reference Library

King's Heath Station from an old postcard circa 1910, with passengers on the Up platform awaiting a suburban train into Birmingham, via Moseley and Camp Hill. An 0-6-0 slowly approaches from the opposite direction, working hard with a goods train at the top of the climb from Camp Hill. A late passenger hurries across the barrow crossing in front of the approaching train, an easier option perhaps than using the footbridge. Passengers could travel in either direction into Birmingham, with up to five trains a day via the Lifford Curve and Bournville. The main service of trains, however, was on the Camp Hill route from King's Norton, with up to 25 trains a day each way. The number of passengers travelling from King's Heath was at its highest between 1876 and 1906, peaking at over 184,000 in the year 1900. From 1907, however, there was a marked reduction, with annual figures as low as 70,000 a year. This was obviously due to the fact that the steam tram service to Birmingham was converted to electric traction in late 1906 and people no doubt preferred this cleaner, cheaper and more direct route into town.

Author's collection

L.M.S.

STRATFORD
ANNUAL MOP FAIR.

EVENING EXCURSION
On SATURDAY, OCT. 12th, 1935
to
STRATFORD-ON-AVON.

From	Depart times.	3rd Cl. Return Fares.
Camp Hill	5.35 p.m.	1/6
Moseley	5.42 p.m.	1/6
Kings Heath	5.46 p.m.	1/3
Kings Norton	5.55 p.m.	1/3
Northfield	6.0 p.m.	1/3
Barnt Green	6.10 p.m.	1/-
Redditch	6.25 p.m.	9d.
Studley	6.35 p.m.	9d.
Alcester	6.48 p.m.	9d.
Broom Junction	7.0 p.m.	9d.

Stratford-on-Avon arrive 7.20 p.m.

The entrance to King's Heath Station at the bottom of the drive leading down from the High Street, as it appeared on 7th November 1961. To the left is the house once occupied by the Station Master and the railway line runs behind it in the cutting. The only other entrance to the station was by means of a pedestrian path which is seen starting behind the Tascos coal office. The path climbed up to the High Street and exited near the Queens Bridge, opposite Valentine Road. *Birmingham Reference Library*

The goods yard looking west from the station drive taken in June 1966. Coal lorries abound in this scene, just a few weeks after the station closed to goods on 2nd May 1966. Modern stores now occupy the site. *R. S. Carpenter*

An 8 ton coal wagon of the type seen at King's Heath Station. F. W. Russell was a coal merchant at King's Heath from 1910 until 1931.

courtesy Phil Coutanche collection

Opposite top: A typical circa 1912 publicity pose showing the coal delivery cart, plastered with advertising posters, of W. Baker & Son, coal merchants, King's Heath, in front of their office in the station drive. Best coal was selling at one shilling and mixed coal at 10d. In the background can be seen the 'Station Pub' in the High Street which was well known to banking engine crews!

courtesy Louis Arthur family

Opposite bottom: Sometime prior to the First World War, Wm. Baker & Sons became Dixon & Baker and the new concern's office is seen here around 1919. It was rather more substantial than most of the coal merchants at King's Heath, being built of brick, whilst the ivy and flower beds lent it an air of bucolic charm. William Baker stands in the doorway and he was shortly to sell the business to Frederick Sharp. Nine horses were regularly used for coal deliveries in the area and were stabled in nearby Grange Road.

courtesy Michael Williams

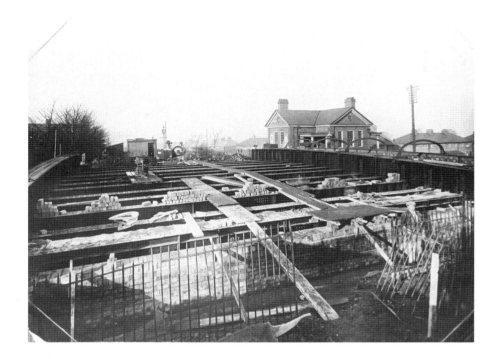

The new Cartland Road bridge being constructed over the railway at Hazelwell Station on 7th December 1928.

Birmingham Reference Library

The new Cartland Road bridge under construction on 7th December 1928, looking towards Hazelwell Station and King's Heath. Hazelwell Signal Box is to the left.

Birmingham Reference Library

Dad's Lane railway bridge midway between King's Heath and Hazelwell stations. The original bridge is seen here being removed on 15th August 1931 as the roads in the area were being widened to cater for the increase in traffic.

Birmingham Reference Library

This view of 15th August 1931 shows the demolition of the original Dad's Lane bridge and illustrates the narrowness of the road and the shortness of the original span. During the planning stages of the building of the line between August and December 1838, the Birmingham & Gloucester Railway encountered some difficulties with land owners in the construction of the line over Dad's Lane. They felt it very desirable to obtain the sanction of the Parish to construct a crossing on the level and to obtain a poll to get consent of the Parishioners. Unfortunately the outcome was not favourable and despite the advanced stage of the works, the Engineer was instructed to lower Dad's Lane and to build a bridge to carry the railway over it.

Birmingham Reference Library

The new Hazelwell Station seen here circa 1907, four years after it had opened and looking towards King's Heath.

Author's collection

Opposite top: A close up of the Up platform buildings around the turn of the century, showing the wonderful array of enamel signs which festooned the waiting rooms.

Author's collection

Opposite bottom: A full complement of King's Heath staff circa 1920, including Signalmen, Booking Office staff, Goods Foreman and Parcels Deliverymen and on the right Station Master Mr. John Brayne.

courtesy Michael Williams

Steam tram near to station 1905.   *Clarence Gilbert collection*

Tram No. 420 on the 39 service from Hill Street via Balsall Heath enters High Street by Valentine Road in April 1947. This route was abandoned in October 1949 and replaced by the extended 48 bus service.   *R. J. Buckley*

— OTHER MEANS OF TRANSPORT —

The first recorded horse bus service from Birmingham to Alcester Lanes End was in 1859. Ten years later in 1869 the Birmingham Omnibus Company was formed with regular services to Moseley. Around 1871 there was a horse drawn omnibus conveyance to Birmingham from the 'King's Arms' Alcester Lanes End five times a day. In 1884 the Birmingham Central Tramways Company Limited started running steam trams to Moseley and in 1887 this service was extended to King's Heath where a depot, coke yard and pits were built in Silver Street. A part of this building has remained in existence for many years since the demise of the steam tram and more recently being the home for 'International Stock'.

In July 1903 the Moseley & King's Heath Journal reported *"A new and improved tram service to King's Heath is now in operation to and from the city. The Moseley Road service now runs through to King's Heath instead of terminating at Moseley Green, the fare for the whole journey being twopence. The new arrangement means a service of five minutes each way"*.

The steam trams finished running, without any special ceremony, on the last day of the lease, 31st December, 1906. The company were then only

Bus 272, built in 1927 is seen passing the Billesley Arms public house on the Outer Circle route circa 1930.

Author's collection

allowed a few hours in which to remove all of their rolling stock which it was said had to be clear of the Birmingham Corporation tracks by 4a.m. I understand that the engines and cars were all driven to the Dudley area for dismantling with the exception of one failed engine and car which remained in the Silver Street Depot until it was taken over by the Birmingham Corporation in 1912.

The electric trams took over all routes on 1st January 1907 and on 29th January the extension to Alcester Lanes End was opened. The 39 and 42 trams were then a familiar site between Alcester Lanes End and town until they were withdrawn on 1st October 1949 with the introduction of the bus services.

A well known bus service passing through King's Heath for many years has been the Outer Circle No. 11. A 1930s booklet advertised. *"A tour of twenty five miles around the outer circle route would take two hours, twenty minutes at a cost of just 15 pence, or about ½d per mile. This rates as the finest ride in the Midlands, if not the whole country."* My mother would often do this tour with her pensioner friends in the 1970s.

Kitson steam engine No. 79 (1893) with Falcon carriage in King's Heath Steam Tram Depot, Silver Street. In this 1895 scene, the tower of King's Heath School can be seen behind the tram.

Clarence Gilbert collection

Staff, including young engine cleaners pose at the Silver Street Tram Depot in 1889. Beyer Peacock engine No. 64 (1886) is being prepared for its next journey.

Clarence Gilbert collection.

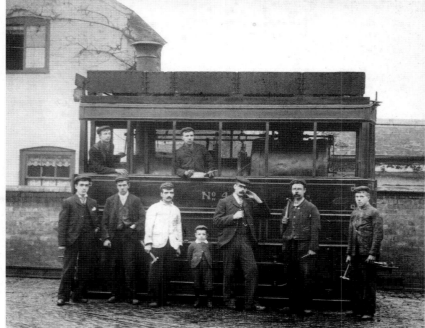

A group of fitters with a rather young apprentice are armed with the tools of their trade at King's Heath Steam Tram Depot in 1900. A cottage in Silver Street is seen behind the locomotive.

Clarence Gilbert collection

Smoke was not allowed to be emitted from the engines but in July of 1892 the following was reported in The Moseley and King's Heath Journal - *"The Birmingham Corporation appear to have some smart officials in their employ, judging from the evidence given at the Police Court recently, in reference to a case in which four tramway engine- drivers in the employ of the Central Tramway Company were summoned for permitting smoke to escape from their engines. The defendants did not deny the charge, but said that the smoke was caused by the quality of the coke they had to burn. Hereupon one of the Company's officials put "the cat among the pigeons" by informing the administrators of the law that the coke was supplied by the Birmingham Corporation! And he ventured to point out very naturally indeed — the anomaly of the Corporation first supplying the fuel, and then prosecuting men for offences caused by their using such fuel. Their worships were considerate enough to fine the unfortunate drivers. I am sorry for the men, but imagine the Corporation have now lost the Central Tramways Company's good graces and future orders".*

A group of some significance pose at Silver Street Tram Depot in 1889.   *Clarence Gilbert collection*

A family group pose in 1895 with Kitson locomotive No. 74 (built 1893) in Silver Street Tram Depot yard.

Clarence Gilbert collection

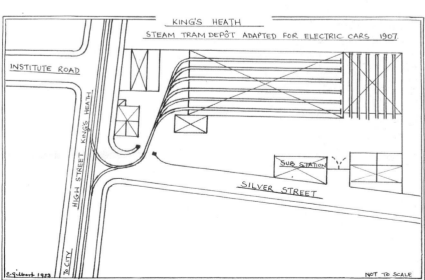

Steam tram depot plan 1907.

Clarence Gilbert collection

Trams 830 and 367 are terminating just short of Alcester Lanes End on 10th July 1949. They are special cars to cater for the King's Heath Dog Track meeting. An approaching bus on the 35 route is about to overtake on its journey to the Maypole.   *T. J. Edgington*

Opposite top: Beyer Peacock steam tram locomotive No. 61 with trailer car by Queens Bridge, King's Heath in 1890.   *Clarence Gilbert collection*

Opposite bottom: One of the last steam trams passes by King's Heath station in 1906, watched by Station Master Mr. Brayne. Mr Brayne is standing by the footpath entrance to the station in the High Street. The tram is running on temporary track whilst work is progressing on laying track in readiness for the new electric tramcars.   *Author's collection*

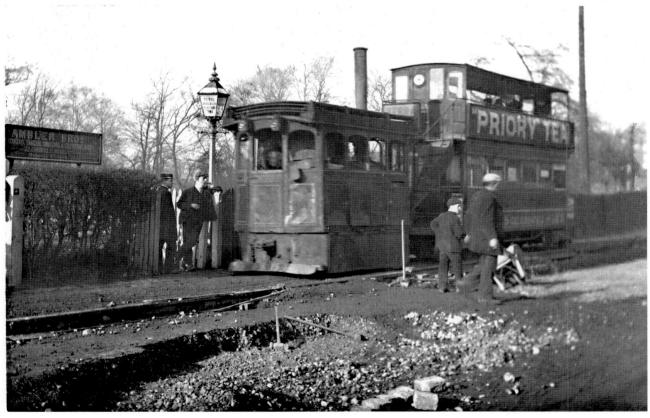

King's Heath Cricket and Football Club c1890 at their ground in Vicarage Road. The club moved to their present home on Alcester Road South in 1927. There was an extraordinary performance in King's Heath's match with Burton on June 10th 1899 when Mr. E. C. Green broke all known records by performing a "hat trick" twice in one innings. King's Heath went in first, and before 5 o' clock they had scored 227 for 8 wickets declared. By ten minutes to six, Burton were all out for 72. In commemoration of the event the K. H. C. C. had the cricket ball mounted in silver and presented to Mr. Green as a souvenir of the "hat trick".   *Birmingham Reference Library*

Children enjoy the gardens and open spaces of Uffculme Park.

courtesy Stan Budd

— Sports & Leisure —

After the demise of the Ideal Cinema in York Road a *Billiards Club* with twelve tables was opened on the site. At the opening in August 1933 an exhibition match took place between England's two leading professionals, Joe Davis and Tom Newman. All male residents of King's Heath were invited to inspect the club with a view to becoming members. The membership for the first year was set at 6d.

A *Baseball Club* was in existence in 1895 although opposition was not easy to find as the sport which was very popular in the States had not yet attracted much interest in the 'old world'. The only other English team at the time played in Liverpool so quite a journey was necessary to meet the opposition.

In the late 19th century social activities in the village were mainly for the male population. *The King's Heath Working Men's Club* was established in 1883 and first started as an Early Morning School in the basement of King's Heath Institute. No alcoholic drinks were provided, the original promoters of the club feeling that it should stand on its merits as a club by promoting fellowship among young men and providing them with an innocent and pure form of recreation. Attractions at this club included billiards, cards, chess, draughts, ping-pong, while an air-gun range, a good library, and a comfortable reading room were provided for the use of members. The club was open to members from 10 a.m. to 10.30 p.m., except Saturdays, when it was open until 11.0 p.m. Early membership was around 150 with the weekly subscription of one penny. A hundred up at billiards cost 4d., fifty up 2d., while 2d was charged for a game of pool or snooker.

The name was changed to the King's Heath Social Club in the 1920s and in 1933 with the sale of the King's Heath Institute, the club moved to new premises in Vicarage Road near to Cartland Road.

From 1926 *greyhound racing* at Alcester Lanes End was also an immediate crowd puller. A 1926 report stated that as many as 6,000 people thronged the stands and grounds. So commodious were the arrangements that the huge crowd could see all there was to be seen without inconvenience. It was popular with all classes and even the fair sex were reported to be turning up in large numbers.

The Dog Track closed in 1971.

Playing *golf* was very popular with folk between the War years. Cocks Moor Woods and Moseley Golf Course in Billesley Lane have for a long time been the main courses in King's Heath, but for a short time in the 1920s and 30s a rival venue came into being at Brandwood House, Brandwood End. In April 1923 the new course was laid out with nine holes and was reported to be a noteworthy example of "private" enterprise. By August 1928 the course had expanded to eighteen sporting holes, the natural contour of which was admirably suited for a first-class course, where all the skill and

patience of the golfer was required. The old Brandwood House had been converted into a modern Club-House, with Lounge, Tea Rooms, Bar, Billiard Rooms, and every convenience. By June 1930 membership had risen to 500 and the proprietors were sparing no expense in improving the course. The district was reported to be very health giving, and people troubled with sluggish liver were said to do well to join the club, with the object of getting rid of their ailments. It was said that the air of Alcester Lanes End was an absolute tonic and the Club House was unequalled by any other club in the Birmingham district. Housing by Dawberry Fields Road now occupies the site of this golf course.

In the 1920s there was also a *Tennis Club* at Brandwood House where the hard and grass courts were said to be in excellent condition. The club was in ideal and healthy surroundings and was handily situated for tram and bus. It was said to be just the place to save doctor's bills! The advert for the golf and tennis club on this page appeared in January 1934.

A number of *football* teams were in existence in the early 1900s and in 1906 members of the Brandwood Rovers F.C. played in the third division of the B. Y. and O. B. league. In October 1914 King's Heath Parish Church F. C. ceased playing owing to players enlisting to serve in Kitchener's new army. Many teams found it necessary to cancel the whole of their fixtures in view of the national crisis.

An *amateur dramatic group* was formed in King's Heath in 1930 calling themselves 'The King's Heath Players'. They appeared regularly at the King's Heath Institute in the 1930s performing mainly comedy plays. In April 1933

Do You Play Golf or Tennis?

Then the

BRANDWOOD HOUSE

GOLF AND TENNIS CLUB
WILL SATISFY ALL YOUR REQUIREMENTS !

THE GOLF CLUB SUBSCRIPTION is Gentlemen, £5 - 5 - 0 ; Ladies, £4 - 4 - 0 per annum. *NO ENTRANCE FEE.*
THE TENNIS CLUB SUBSCRIPTION is now only £1 - 1 - 0 per annum.
Green Fees 1/6 per day, 3/- Saturdays, Sundays and Bank Holidays.
Everything possible has been done by Mr. Roberts to make the Golf Links and Tennis Courts as near perfection as possible.

BRANDWOOD ROAD, ALCESTER LANES END.

BRANDWOOD ROAD, ALCESTER LANES END.

Telephone : SOUTH 1055.

Opposite bottom: A photograph by A. E. Dawson of Station Road, King's Heath shows two unidentified local football teams. One team in an Aston Villa type kit and the other sporting a galleon or sailing ship badge on the shirt. *Author's collection*

An early post card view of a Women's Hockey team possibly in King's Heath Park. *Author's collection*

King's Heath Tug-o-War team display their haul of trophies c1912. On Whit Monday of this year
the team were reported in the local journal as competing in the Road and Path Sports at Redditch.
*"They appeared to be a formidable set of men and for a time it seemed they would carry all before them.
They won all their semi-finals, but were at last beaten in the final by a team of Midland Railway giants".*

Author's collection

King's Heath Tug-o-War team in action, circa 1912.   *Author's collection*

the company presented Frederick Lonsdale's famous comedy "The Last of Mrs. Cheyney". The play was very well supported, the hall of the King's Heath Institute being filled by the audience. The comedy was given in aid of the Lord Mayor's Distress Fund and was under the patronage of the Right Worshipful Lord Mayor of Birmingham.

The King's Heath Observer of 13th November 1936 went on to say *"The splendid progress The King's Heath Players have made is something of which the King's Heath people should be proud. This is the sixth year of the Players and the next production will be the 13th, so they have maintained an average of just over two productions a year"*. The Players were affiliated to the Birmingham Amateur Dramatic Federation.

The First World War gave a big fillip to the **allotment** movement, and in order to assist in maintaining the food supply, local authorities were given wide powers to enter upon any unoccupied land without consent, or if occupied, with the consent of the occupier and land-lord, and either cultivate the land themselves or let it for cultivation. The immediate demand for allotments was enormous with no fewer than 13,274 plots in Birmingham being laid out as a war-time measure.

In 1938, the number of allotments under the control of the Corporation was about 12,224, on 147 sites, mainly on the outskirts of the city, and King's Heath had its fair share of these. At this time there were also about 2,000 allotments let by private owners.

During the Second World War allotments were deemed necessary again and the 'Dig for Victory' slogan was adopted. I have vivid childhood memories of my father taking me on the cross-bar of his bike to his allotment plot on the site later occupied by the Swanshurst Girls School. Another plot close to my home was the one in Addison Road which for many years was famous for its prize winning exhibits at various Horticultural Shows.

Cinemas were very popular before the television era arrived and the first picture house in King's Heath was at Ruskin Hall, 25, Institute Road. It opened in 1911, the proprietors being King's Heath Electric Pictures Ltd. It was also known as the 'King's Heath Picture Palace' and even changed its name to the 'Cosy Cinema' in 1915 prior to its eventual closure.

A news item in June 1912 stated - "'King's Heath Picture Palace'. *This house has been redecorated and is now under new management. There have recently been some very interesting pictures shown here, which have included: "The King Reviewing the Fleet at Portland, etc."*

In September 1912 a newspaper reported *"This beautiful little Picture House, situated in Institute Road, King's Heath, continues to draw large audiences nightly to view the beautiful sets of pictures shown. The shows here are of an entertaining and often educational character, and the management know how to cater equally well for children and adults. Coupled with all this is the fact that the building itself is well equipped and furnished and one can sit in comfort and ease throughout the evenings entertainment. The programme is changed on Mondays and Thursdays and films illustrating the current views of the world form an important feature of each performance. Specially large audiences were present during the week commencing August 12th to witness the re-production of the King's Heath Allotment Association Show, and most realistic it was"*.

A February 1913 issue reported. *"The management of the King's Heath Picture House, Institute Road, is nothing if not "smart," since the Second Round of the English Cup, played on February 1st, and featuring Villa v. West Ham, was shown to their patrons on the following Monday. Rising rates do not adversely affect the fortunes of this go-ahead theatre, for packed houses are the rule. This is mainly due to the uniform excellence of the programmes, nothing "dull" being given a place"*.

With the opening of the 'Ideal Picture House', High Street on 5th February 1913 a noticeable drop in numbers was evident at the 'King's Heath Picture House'.

A March 1913 news item reported *"In spite of business opposition, this splendid Picture House in*

Institute Road continues to hold its own in popularity and in the high-class nature of its "shows." The quality of the films exhibited is always of the best; attractive, educational, and amusing subjects are portrayed with life-like reality, while the whole of the entertainments contain nothing of a questionable nature. Personal comfort of patrons is also studied in every possible way".

The 'King's Heath Picture House' struggled on but could not compete with the new cinema in High Street and finally closed its doors in 1915.

In 1928 the Kelly's Directory listed the building as being the Moseley Masonic Hall Co. Ltd. It later became the Gas Show Room Building. The history of the 'Ideal' and the 'Kingsway' is mentioned on pages 60 and 63.

The Tudor Picture House in Haunch Lane opened on 30th March 1929 with a seating capacity of 1,000. After closure on Saturday 17th March 1962 the cinema was used as a Social Centre and Bingo Club. It has more recently been demolished to make way for the building of retirement homes.   *Birmingham Reference Library*

Opposite bottom: The Birmingham Corporation Tramways Department Sports Day at the Wheelers Lane Sports Ground in July 1912. Mrs A Baker is seen presenting one of the trophies and the General Manager of the Tramways Department, Mr. Alfred Baker is seated alongside sporting a straw hat. Only four years previously in 1908 the Birmingham Tramways Athletic Club had secured the field of twelve or thirteen acres as a playing field. The King's Heath Observer of 7th July 1933 wrote *"There were no less than 3,000 visitors to the Tramways Stadium on Wednesday of last week, when the 26th Annual Amateur Athletic Festival and Fancy Dress Carnival was held"*. I have fond memories of attending these events as a child and watching the thrilling cycle track races featuring the likes of Tommy Godwin and other top cyclists.   *Author's collection*

A group of Girl Guides photographed in the King's Heath area by Albert Edward Dawson circa 1914.

Author's collection

The swimming baths in Institute Road were opened on 18th August 1923. At the time they were said to be of the most modern design with the latest filtration system and water purification plant. The water always had a clear appearance and by its transparency was said to aid rescuers if swimmers got into difficulties. There was just one pool which was 100 feet long by 35 feet wide. There were also 40 private washing baths of which 20 were reserved for women. These washing baths were occasionally used by our family. The alternative would be to get the tin bath off the nail in the coal shed and have a bath in the kitchen!

Collapsible dressing rooms were provided which when removed would allow spectators at special events. The bath could also be boarded over at certain sessions and was let for dances and other social gatherings. The first whist drive and dance in connection with the King's Heath Swimming Club was held on 24th November 1923 when upwards of 350 members attended. On 17th February 1934 a Fancy Dress Ball was held and prizes for the best and most original costumes were awarded and presented by Jack Hood, the European Boxing Welter Weight Champion. The Lawrence Dance Orchestra performed regularly for dances at the baths in the 1930s.

These conventional baths were closed in 1987 and swimming facilities are now housed at the Cocksmoor Leisure Centre near Alcester Lanes End. What a pity these conventional swimming bath facilities were lost to King's Heathens! *Birmingham Reference Library*

101

King's Heath Swimming Club's winning Water Polo Team of 1927. Another photograph by Albert Edward Dawson.

Author's collection

This is the inside of the King's Heath Baths at the time of opening in 1923.

Birmingham Reference Library

King's Heath Adult School Band proudly pose for the camera of Albert Edward Dawson circa 1912. The band was formed in 1906 and according to the local press was still performing well into the 1930s, as evidenced by the advert below which appeared in May 1934.   *Author's collection*

The Adult School Prize Band
KING'S HEATH

Headquarters : *Council Schools, King's Heath.*

Prize Winners : Crystal Palace, Bournville, Redditch, Chasetown, Tenbury, Halesowen, Blackheath.

OPEN FOR ENGAGEMENTS

Applications to—
G. ROGERS, 9 Avenue Rd., King's Heath.

The Adult School Brass Band was formed in early 1906 and on 5th February a social gathering was held at the King's Heath Baptist School Room to celebrate its successful formation. The band played an important part in the social life of King's Heath and there were a number of successful appeals for funds to pay for new instruments and uniforms. Substantial donations were received from prominent local public men including The Right Hon. Joseph Chamberlain M.P. and Major G. H. Cartland.

In June 1908 Empire Day was publicly celebrated at King's Heath amid general rejoicings. The King's Heath Brass Band, together with the bugle band of All Saints' Company of the Church Lads Brigade, marched through the principal streets prior to the ceremony.

In the 1930s the band regularly performed for the occasion of the St. Dunstan's Annual Fete, which was held in the grounds of 'Kingsfield'.

NO 6. CROOK. SERIES.   K. H. BAND.
KINGS HEATH PARK.   COPYRIGHT.

A large crowd relaxes in King's Heath Park as the band performs under the stand nearby. King's Heath was without a park until 1908 when the Local Government Board sanctioned the purchase of King's Heath House for the purpose of a public park, at a cost of £12,500. £1,000 of this was taken to be the value of the house. The new park was fifteen acres in extent and possessed an ornamental lake. This view circa June 1909 shows the new popularity of the park following the introduction of three new tennis courts which were being well patronised. The park presented an attractive appearance with its fine show of rhododendron blooms and during this time regular pierrot concerts were also a feature. The park has retained its horticultural interest over the years and still holds annual flower shows to this day. The BBC Gardening programmes were also broadcasted live from the park.

Author's collection

104

Regarding the lack of a park the Moseley & King's Heath Society Journal of June 1907 reported *"Selly Oak has its park, Stirchley has come into possession of twelve and a half acres of public ground, but King's Heath, as usual, is all forlorn. Meanwhile the children play in the bye-roads, and the youths disport themselves at cricket on the waste ground near King's Heath Institute. King's Heath and the adjoining district of Moseley possess in themselves many natural beauties, but notwithstanding this a public park would come as a boon to many".*

The Rose Garden, King's Heath Park, recently planted around the time of the First World War.   *Author's collection*

King's Heath House in the park was used as a refugee home during the First World War. It was in later years home for the Horticultural School.

Birmingham Reference Library

King's Heath May Festival group taken in the Institute Road School yard, 1933.

courtesy Stan Budd

Comely's shop at 135 High Street was a library but also doubled up as a needlecraft shop and sold wools for knitting. The lady to the left of the doorway in this circa 1912 photograph is Lillian Gilbert who helped run the business, the library being first listed at this address in 1910.   *David Lukeman*

KINGS HEATH
HORSE SHOW
WHIT-MONDAY, 6th JUNE, 1938

SHOW OPENS at 10-0 a.m.

Trams : Nos 39, 42, and 51 ; and Buses Nos. 17 and 35 pass the Ground.

ALCESTER LANES END TRAM TERMINUS

Classes for
HUNTERS. — CHILDREN — TRADESMEN — MOUNTED COMPETITIONS

The King's Heath Show, which was established in 1898, became a popular event for many years. The show was initially held at Highbury, the home of Joseph Chamberlain and after four successful years transferred to the Priory in Vicarage Road, the home of Major J. Howard Cartland before returning again to Highbury in 1908.

The show went from strength to strength, becoming so successful that in 1923 the organisers bought land at Alcester Lanes End and constructed their own showground. It not only accommodated the horse show but also had a stadium. It became the venue for athletics, flower shows and tennis, football and cricket matches. Three years later the centre was converted into a greyhound stadium.

In June 1932 The Moseley & King's Heath Society Journal reported *"Between three and four thousand people attended the 29th Annual Show which took place at Alcester Lanes End on Whit Monday. Despite unfavourable weather the Society scored another success, for the entries were numerically good, and the class of exhibits was on the high plane usually associated with this event"*.

Except during the war years the Annual Show was still held at Alcester Lanes End until 1965. So popular was the show that sometimes the turnstiles had to be closed in the interests of safety.

When Cocks Moors Woods was extended, the Society bought a 22 acre site at Earlswood to make King's Heath Horse Show the oldest local event. Houses have since been built on the Alcester Lanes End site.

BIRMINGHAM
Torchlight Tattoo.

ORGANISED BY THE WARWICKSHIRE TERRITORIAL ARMY ASSOCIATION IN AID OF MILITARY CHARITIES MAY 3RD–15TH 1926

Kings Heath Horse Show Grounds.

Programme   -   Price Sixpence.

MARTIN BILLING, SON & CO., PRINTERS, B'HAM.

The committee of important looking gentlemen at the King's Heath Horse Show, Alcester Lanes
End on Whit Monday 17th May 1937.   *Author's collection*

The Rawling's Bros. entry at the King's Heath Horse Show Whit Monday 1955.

Author's collection

Group 10 children outside the Infant Block at Colmore Road Primary School around the time of the First World War. Note the houses in Colmore Road were not yet built. This is another A. E. Dawson of Station Road photograph.

Author's collection

A First World War scene of Colmore Road School in use as a War Hospital. It was in fact an annex of the 1st Southern General War Hospital at the University. The children from the school were taught at King's Heath School during this period.

courtesy Stan Budd

— EDUCATION —

The earliest mention of a school in King's Heath was in 1846. The school for infants became a National School in 1870 and was open for boys and girls with John Corbett as Master.

The Board Schools were built in 1878 on the site of what is now "Scots Corner" and stretched from opposite Silver Street on the High Street to well down what is now Institute Road. It was built of red brick, with stone dressings by the King's Norton School Board, from the designs of Mr William Hale, architect to accommodate 150 boys, 150 girls and 220 Infants. The overall cost including the site and furniture etc amounted to over £7,000.

By 1885 the village had attained considerably larger proportions, and at a cost of nearly £2,000 the schools were enlarged, thereby increasing the accommodation to 749. In 1890 the schools held 260 boys, 240 girls and 221 infants with attendances reported to have been around 100%, a figure which is probably rather exaggerated.

In 1893, the Board were called upon by the Education Department to again enlarge the schools. This enlargement consisted of erecting a new infant school and alterating the old infants departments, so as to adapt it to the requirements of a junior mixed school, the new building being divided into three class rooms, each containing accommodation for sixty children on the dual desk system.

In 1904 the school was now under the King's Norton and Northfield Urban District Council Education Committee and the number of children on roll had risen to 1,602 with an average attendance of 1559. By 1911 however, the average attendance had dropped alarmingly to 1,211. Around this time because of possible overcrowding, two new temporary schools came into being. King's Heath House in Vicarage Road opened in 1909 with 306 infants on roll (average attendance 267) and Grove Road (mixed) for 293 children (average attendance 262). This temporary school had opened in 1909 to provide education for children in the Urban District who had formerly attended Birmingham schools since King's Norton and Northfield had refused to pay Birmingham for their education. Both these temporary schools closed in 1911 with the opening of Colmore Road Council School.

The King's Heath school site was altered and re-organised in 1915 for boys, girls and infants and in 1928-30 for Senior Boys, Junior Mixed and Infants. The site was enlarged in 1934 but closed in 1939 on the opening of Wheelers Lane Council School. The old 1895 Infant block re-opened in 1949, the other block was later repaired and re-opened in 1951 for Junior mixed, with the Infants remaining in the smaller block. The Institute Road site finally closed in September 1982 when the new modern school was built in Valentine Road.

The new Wheelers Lane School was built in 1938 and opened in 1939 with the Boys County Modern School becoming a separate school in 1945.

Away from King's Heath, the Billesley Council School opened in 1925 with open-air classrooms fitted with screens and heating supplied from pipes under the floor, and was the model for twelve other schools.

Perhaps the oldest school in the area was at Yardley Wood, where a temporary Board School had opened in 1838 in leasehold buildings also used as a church, having been erected in 1828 as a meeting house. In 1846 there were 58 boys and girls on the register with a master and a mistress. It closed and opened again in the 1880's but then closed in 1893 on the opening of Yardley Wood Board School.

Children pose for the camera at the King's Heath Infants Parents Day of 1935.   *courtesy Stan Budd*

Group 3 pupils at Kings Heath School circa 1902.   *David Lukeman*

King's Heath School (Institute Road) football shield winners, 1937-8   *courtesy Stan Budd*

Wheelers Lane Junior School leavers pose for the camera in 1949 with Head Teacher, Mr Flavell. Mr. Flavell (1900-1982) retired in 1962 and lived nearby in Haunch Lane. I am sixth from the left on the back row.

Author's collection

advert from
March 1937

A group of pupils in their brown and yellow uniforms at the King's Heath High School, Alcester Road South in 1947. The photograph was supplied by Kate Keown, née Sumner, who is seated in the middle of the front row. The school which at one time operated in the Moseley and King's Heath Institute is now but a memory.

courtesy Kate Keown

Another view of pupils at King's Heath School at their May Festival event.

courtesy Stan Budd

A group of children at King's Heath School perform the Maypole Dance. This postcard view was sent to Preston, Lancashire from King's Heath on May 2nd 1905.

Author's collection

The Billesley Arms Hotel built in 1854 by Benjamin Sawyer, looking towards King's Heath.

Author's collection

Bar Staff at the Billesley Arms Hotel.

Author's collection

— BREWERY & PUBLIC HOUSES —

This artist's impression of the King's Heath Brewery shows the vastness of the site following its take over by The Birmingham Breweries Ltd in 1895. This is supposedly a copy from an actual picture of the brewery site that hung on the wall of the offices. In the 1830s the Bate family of the 'Cross Guns' set up the brewery in King's Heath in order to supply their own pub. In rate books from the 1860s it was known as "Isaac Bate and Company, The King's Heath Brewery" and remained so until 1888. It was then known as: "F. Everitt and Company. (Est. 1831) late Isaac Bate and Company." Finally, by 1896 it was known as: "Birmingham Breweries Limited".

In 1902 Birmingham Breweries Limited and the 'Cross Guns' were purchased by Mitchells and Butlers for £16,715. The brewery was left derelict and finally demolished in 1903-4.

The artesian well that served the brewery is still in existence. It is situated underneath the kerbstones opposite the first house on the right hand side of Bank Street (looking from High Street). It was sunk to a depth of 1,000 feet, with a bore of 10 inches in diameter and lined with copper pipes. The brickwork of the well, which extends for only 15 feet down from the surface, was filled in when Bank Street was made, but a slab was placed over the actual bore so that if required, it could be re-opened. Such is the well today, over 50 years later, though the possibility now of the water ever being drawn from it again, is very remote.

photograph courtesy Peter Topley

The 'Cross Guns' with the King's Heath Brewery behind. The original pub which at this time is advertising Pool and Billiards was built around 1792 when two cottages were converted to make one large building. This building was dominated by a large pear tree which was growing right across its front. This tree is reported to have been planted in 1788 shortly before the building was converted to an Inn and in the early years the Inn was often referred to by the locals as "The Pear Tree".

The 'Cross Guns' was licensed in 1831 and an interesting fact is that the commodious smoke-room and the room over it were built as part of the inn, for the express purpose of the Police Court! The magistrates thus had the privilege of the opportunity of partaking of a drop of "Scotch" and other refreshments. Prisoners were removed to cells in the village, at the corner of Balaclava Street.

During the 1860s James and Isaac Bates's brewing exploits must have made them very wealthy indeed. With their new found wealth they further consolidated their monopoly on the brewing and sale of beer in King's Heath. In 1866 they purchased the 'Hare and Hounds' pub and its associated land outright. This meant that they owned two pubs and a brewery right at the heart of King's Heath.

In 1881 The 'Cross Guns' and brewery were purchased by Frederick Everitt and Company who later sold it to Birmingham Breweries Limited. In 1896 it was decided that the old 'Cross Guns' was no longer big enough or modern enough to effectively serve the community of King's Heath anymore. The old pub was replaced with a much grander building in 1897. In 1898 a new billiard room was added on the first floor over the old stable which was turned into a large smoke room. The 'Cross Guns' became a Mitchells and Butlers managed house and remained so until the 1990s when it was renamed 'The Goose and Granite' and more latterly 'The Goose'.

Author's collection

Another view of the earlier Cross Guns circa 1897 with brewery behind and famous pear tree. An interesting fact is that this specimen of horticulture was planted as early as 1788. Note also the gents' urinal to the left.

- courtesy Stan Budd

The rebuilt 'Cross Guns' at the corner of Bank Street from a postcard sent to Glasgow on October 31st 1907. In more modern times it has been renamed 'The Goose'.

Author's collection

Edward Collins and his wife Eleanor proudly stand in front of the 'Hare and Hounds Hotel' soon after taking over the establishment from Levi Cotttrell in 1895. The Collins family ran the hotel until 1906.

The 'Hare and Hounds' was built between 1824 and 1828 by Aaron Payton, bricklayer of King's Heath. He had bought the parcel of land with James Bate, gunlock maker and owner of the 'Cross Guns'. Aaron, who was born in 1877, lived initially in Moseley and learned a trade as a bricklayer. The move with his family to King's Heath by 1821 was a logical one as the area had a clay soil perfect for brick making. The village was also beginning to grow with the new buildings springing up from these locally made bricks.

The original pub had bay windows fronting onto the Turnpike Road but the adjoining building on the corner of what would later be York Road had various different uses.

In fact in a deed dated 1843 it was described as being in use as a Police Station in the use of the Worcestershire Rural Police. Therefore, Aaron Payton not only built the 'Hare and Hounds' public house on his land, but also the first recorded Police station in King's Heath. When Aaron left the 'Hare and Hounds' the agreement with the police was obviously discontinued although in the 1851 census the adjacent house was listed as being the residence where the superintendent of Police lived with his family and a Police constable.

The original 'Hare and Hounds' was demolished in 1906 with the new structure being completed by July 1907. The new 'Hare and Hounds' was eventually bought by the Holt Brewery Company in 1910 and this brought an end to the 'Hare and Hounds' independence. It would now be continually owned by large Brewery Companies and run by their tenant managers. Different refurbishments have been made over the years but the interior has retained many of its original features to this day, meriting as a result, being listed as a Grade ll listed building on August 24th 1995. *photograph courtesy Stan Budd*

This earlier picture of the 'Hare and Hounds' is circa 1895. The Inn is the taller building in the centre with the bay windows. The house adjoining it to the left had various occupants including a policeman and a dairyman. *courtesy Stan Budd*

The rebuilt 'Hare and Hounds' c1912 from a postcard view. The clock at this time was still in working order. *Author's collection*

Highbury, a well known establishment in use as a temporary hospital for the wounded during the First World War .This view is on a postcard sent from Highbury on July 24th 1916. The writer says *"What do you think of my abode? I must be getting high up in the world, a change to sand bags!"*   *Author's collection*

— FAMOUS PEOPLE & HOUSES —

A photographic post card of The Right Hon Joseph Chamberlain, M. P. outside Highbury at the turn of the century. The photograph was taken by George Hynd, a prominent King's Heath photographer.

Author's collection

Opposite: The Rhododendron Beds in the grounds of Highbury. This view was on a post card sent to Llandudno Junction in 1912.

Author's collection

Kingsfield House was the home of Joseph Henry Nettlefold until his death in 1881. In 1886 Alban Gardner Buller J.P., Solicitor and Wesleyan, made his home there until his death in 1924. In the King's Heath Observer of 11th November 1932, St Dunstan's High School for Boys and Girls under Ten, conducted by the Sisters of St. Paul, Selly Park were operating from Kingsfield House. Later, in the 1950s, Bishop Challoner R. C. School was built on the site of the house and in 1964 St Dunstan's R. C. Primary School was built on the site of what was Kingsfield House orchard.   *Author's collection*

The Library, St. Johns Hall, Highbury.   *Mike Rhodes collection*

— POLICE & FIRE SERVICES —

A 1907 gathering of Police Officers inside the courtyard of King's Heath Police Station. *courtesy Stan Budd*

In the 1800s the police did not have the luxury of a large station to operate from and about the year 1840 prisoners arrested in this district were tried sometimes at the 'Cross Guns' public house, and at other times at the 'King's Arms', Alcester Lanes End. The prisoners were sometimes to be seen chained to the fire-grate at the 'King's Arms' public house, apparently as the only most convenient place of safety.

Between 1842-9, the building next to the 'Hare and Hounds' was used as a police station and a deed dated 1843 reads *"All that other messuage tenement or dwellinghouse lately erected and built by the said A. Payton as aforementioned with the outbuildings thereto belonging and then used as a Police Station."* This particular building is recorded in the use of the Worcestershire Rural Police and the stocks and whipping post were opposite. A portion of the 'Hare and Hounds' was built upon the site of the old police station and York Road was built upon the old police station yard. Brum Lawrence had the honour of being the last man to occupy the stocks.

The 1851 census lists this building as being the residence where the superintendent of Police, George Graham, (31), lived with his family and a Police constable by the name of Charles Rodman. In 1852 two rooms were built onto the 'Cross Guns' for the express purpose of a Police Court.

Around 1866 the Police Force consisted of Superintendent Humphries and a constable named Tandy, neither of whom possessed uniforms. . The police station was afterwards removed to Balaclava Road, just previous to the erection of the present police station.

Special Constables, Mr England and The Reverend M. W. Smith (Curate at All Saints Church 1913-15).

courtesy Stan Budd

King's Heath Fire & Ambulance Station, Silver Street in the 1950s. The Fire Station was established in King's Heath in 1886 and in 1892 the Volunteer Brigade consisted of 2 Officers and 9 men. In 1911 this had risen to 23 men with one steam and one manual engine. In 1893 the King's Heath Brigade won first prize in the manual engine driving competition. The location of the Fire Station in Silver Street varied over the years, in 1896 being on the right hand side between Nos. 14 and 16 but in 1900 it was next to No. 58. In 1901 it was next to 108 then from 1902 until 1924 the service operated from next to 88 Silver Street. Its final position from 1925 until its closure was on the left hand side between 15 and 25 Silver Street. *Author's collection*

A 1960s view of the Silver Street Fire Station and two engines.

Mike Trueman

The Wesleyan Church in Cambridge Road.

The foundation stone for the church was laid on 23rd June 1896, in the presence of a large concourse of people. It was opened for worship by the then President of the Conference, the Rev. W. L. Watkinson, on Friday, January 22, 1898. The new church, which cost £7,710 to build, was erected of red terra-cotta and brick, in the Early English Gothic style of architecture. It would seat 620 persons and be 80 feet long by 49 feet wide internally, and 42 feet high to the top of the ridge. It was divided into nave and aisles by three wide arches on each side, supported by quatrefoil-shaped polished red Aberdeen granite piers, having doulting stone caps and bases. It had a tower and spire, the top being 120 feet above the ground. The main entrance was from School Road and in 1940 there were two attached school halls and nine ancillary rooms.

Prior to the building of the church, a chapel existed on the site. This building was erected in 1888 at a cost of upwards of £2,000 from designs by Mr. W. Hale, architect. The seating accommodation was for about 230 persons. The residents of King's Heath belonging to this denomination previous to the year 1887, worshipped in the Board Schools.

Mike Rhodes collection

– Churches –

All Saints Church 1875.

The church has been a focal land mark in the village for almost 150 years and this early view shows the attractive original roof tiles laid in a diaper pattern. For some time previous to the erection of the church, divine service was regularly celebrated in the schoolroom, but, owing to a lack of space, it was determined in 1859 to erect a church capable of accommodating 430 persons. The cost of this would be £2,750 and towards this sum upwards of £1,500 was promised by the inhabitants and landowners of the district plus a similar amount from other donations. The church was designed by F. Preedy in the perpendicular style consisting of a chancel, nave, south aisle and a square tower with pinnacles at its angles and a lofty spire. The laying of the foundation stone took place on 27th April 1859, in the presence of a very numerous company. A procession was formed at the schools and led by the churchwardens and John

Cartland. The choir and the school children then proceeded to the site of the church. The foundation stone was laid by Mr. Foley on behalf of Miss Taylor and a collection was made, amounting to upwards of £60. The school children were afterwards regaled with buns, etc and the workmen employed were supplied with a substantial dinner. The spire was not added to the tower until 1866 owing to the initial lack of funds. A brass plate was fixed in the east end of the nave which sets forth the fact that the foundation stone was laid by "Ann Elizabeth Taylor, only daughter of the late John Taylor, Esq., of Moseley Hall,

on Wednesday of Easter week, April 27th, 1859."

The appearance of the church was agreeably changed and greatly improved in 1882 by the addition of a north aisle, organ chamber and vestries. The accommodation afforded by the new aisle had the effect of providing 127 extra sittings.

In August 1893, a chancel screen was erected by the members of the Cartland family, in memory of the late Mr. and Mrs John Cartland, the screen being made entirely of wrought-iron in the Renaissance of Gothic styles.   *Birmingham Reference Library*

Baptist Church, High Street circa 1910.

The Baptist church was founded in 1811 when a group of lay preachers held meetings in a small cottage in the then truly rural village of King's Heath. For six years the cottage meetings were regularly held, when it became necessary to provide larger and more convenient accommodation for the increasing congregation. The General Baptist Meeting House was thereupon erected partly on the site of the present

structure in 1815 and was opened in 1816. This building lasted until 1872, when falling into a very dilapidated state it was deemed quite unsuitable for divine worship. A restored building was constructed in 1872 and in 1892 the main Sunday service attracted a congregation of 279.

So prosperous did the work become in church and school alike, that in 1895, it was decided to build the present commodious premises. Subscriptions were raised, and on Sunday, 21st March 1897, services were held for the last time in the ivy-fronted building prior to its demolition. The foundation stones were laid on 15th September 1897 and the church eventually opened on Wednesday 4th May 1898. The new church cost £7,000 to build and was described as being situated on the High Street (formerly called Alcester Road), partly on the site of the old chapel and partly on the ground occupied by two ancient cottages. It was built to accommodate 550 worshippers and erected in the modern Gothic style of architecture, the materials used being Leicestershire bricks, with Hollingstone stone for the dressings, and the mullions of the windows. The church building scheme was completed with the exception of the tower and spire which were to be added when funds became available.

In 1916 the church was said to have done good service in throwing open their Sunday schools as rest rooms for wounded soldiers. The premises were comfortably furnished and provided with books and papers, with light refreshments being served to the 'Tommies'. On one day alone 431 men attended and were served with refreshments.

On 15th July 1917 the 106th Anniversary of the Baptist 'cause' in King's Heath was celebrated at the High Street church. The original church services were first conducted in 1811, though it was believed that as far back as 1791 services were held in a private house, the property of Mr. William Piddock, and inhabited by Mr. John Harwood, a member of the Baptist community. Authentic records of the church prove it to have been started by a number of laymen attached to the old Lombard Street Baptist Church, who held meetings in a small cottage.

The Boys' Brigade 6th Birmingham Company was based at the church and I spent many happy years of my youth as a member there in the 1950s being a drummer in the band, parading in the streets on a Sunday and attending annual camps - happy days. The Girls Life Brigade also operated from the church.

In the 1950s the Baptist Sunday School rooms were being used as classrooms for Wheelers Lane Boys School. The School log book of September 8th 1950 reported *"Two of the fifteen forms are now housed in the Baptist School Room, High Street with Mr. Bonner (1.2) and Mr. Jones (1.1)(3rd post) in charge"*. This was obviously found necessary due to lack of space at the main school.   *Birmingham Reference Library*

A Sunday School teachers and pupils group outside the Christadelphian Church in Institute Road circa 1905. There was a Monumental Stone Masons to the left of the church at this time and Wraggs are still running a similar business there today.
courtesy Christadelphian church

Other places of worship

After 1860, new chapels began to appear in the suburbs at an increasing rate. The period of most intensive building seems to have been the fourteen years between 1875 and 1888. Between 1871 and 1901 new centres of population came into being in areas inadequately served by existing chapels. At this time the population of King's Norton, King's Heath and Moseley considered together rose from less than 10,000 to 37,000.

In 1904 there was a Wesleyan Mission Hall in King's Road and the Bible Christian Methodist Church in Addison Road. In 1911 this was listed as being the United Methodist Chapel.

The Bethany Mission House, King's Road was opened in 1912 with an association with St Mary Magdalen Mission Hall. This was then replaced in 1916 by the consecrated church of St Mary Magdalen, Hazelwell. The foundation stone of the new Church Mission Room was laid on 6th December 1915 by Miss Cartland.

Another prominent King's Heath church is St Dunstan's R. C. which was initially opened on the corner of Station Road and Westfield Road on the 19th December 1896. This corrugated iron church was 80 feet long by 33 feet wide and afforded accommodation for 200 worshippers. The church was destroyed by bombing in 1941 and services were held in various places until the new church hall, serving as a chapel opened during 1953 in Kingsfield Road. This when originally built was a simple rectangular brick building with pre-cast stone windows, having a projected Lady Chapel on the south side.

A group of young soldiers are on parade at the rear of a large church in the King's Heath area.

Author's collection

Opposite: A family group outside a church in the King's Heath area.

Author's collection

Albert Edward Dawson was a well known local photographer taking pictures of local scenes and events around King's Heath for many years. He also provided the images for many of the postcards that were produced of the area in the early 1900s, some of which appear in this book. He was born in 1864 and appeared to operate for all of his business life from his home in Station Road until his death in 1934.

The family link was retained in Station Road until recently with the established Dawson Timber Mills plying their trade.

A number of postcards taken by A. E. Dawson are still turning up at postcard fairs but there are not many which state the location or the occasion. Some of these have been included in the book in the hope that someone may recognise the location, such as the two photographs on this and the previous pages of events at churches. I would be very pleased to find some answers.

The old cottages in Billesley Lane (formally Bulley Lane) in 1912.

Author's collection

Billesley Lane in 1910. The young ladies in the picture are L to R Ethel Smith, a maid, Winnie, and Gertrude and Marjorie Everton who came from Moseley Village. Behind the tree in the centre was the blacksmith's forge.

Author's collection

—BILLESLEY, YARDLEY WOOD, & HAPPY VALLEY —

The parade of shops on the Yardley Wood Road near to Brook Lane in 1958.

Author's collection

Swanshurst Park and pool.

Author's collection

Children play happily by the water below the aqueduct carrying the Stratford on Avon canal at Yardley Wood.

Author's collection

The ford in the valley at Yardley Wood. The sign further up the hill says *'This way to the pleasure boats'* (on the canal at Happy Valley).

Author's collection

A winter view c1912 of the 'Four Arches' bridge looking across the River Cole towards Brook Farm. The continuation of Brook Lane at this time used to pass by the bridge until it was straightened out in the 1930s. Colebourne Road and Coleside Avenue now occupy the site of the original lane. *Author's collection*

A bus with outside stairway waits for passengers at the junction of Priory Road and School Road. *Author's collection*

A 1912 scene of the ford at Scribers Lane, Yardley Wood. The North Warwickshire Railway line which was built a few years earlier can just be seen behind the trees. The writer of the card says *"We are five miles out of Birmingham so have a long walk to town in the morning".*   *Author's collection*

A peaceful Slade Lane looking across Cole Brook towards the railway embankment.

Author's collection

Tritterford Mill, also known as Titterford Mill or Yardley Wood Mill, near to the junction of where Trittiford Road now meets Priory Road.

Author's collection

Yardley Wood Mill was also shown as a steel mill on the 1884 Ordinance Survey maps.

Author's collection

Yardley Wood Windmill near the pond off what is now Windmill Road. This view is looking from the High Street.
Author's collection

'The Haven' public house, School Road, Yardley Wood. The pub had various name changes before it succumbed to the demolition men to make way for residential flats.
Author's collection

Another posed shot in Yardley Wood, possibly at the bottom of School Road judging by the lie of the land.

Author's collection

A group pose for the cameraman in Yardley Wood, possibly in School Road. The postcard was sent from 'Drakes Crossing' in July 1912.

Author's collection

Yardley Wood Station. N. Warwickshire Rly. R(B'm)Ld.

196. YARDLEY WOOD STATION, G.W.R.

Passengers await their train at Yardley Wood Station in April 1957 while tank loco 5107 heads towards the City.

Real photograph Co. Ltd.

Opposite top: Yardley Wood Station, known as Yardley Wood Platform until 1924. This view from a post card is taken shortly after the opening of the North Warwickshire line in 1908 and is looking towards Stratford-on-Avon. *Author's collection*

Opposite bottom: Yardley Wood Station taken shortly after opening in 1908. This view is taken from Highfield Road, looking over the original narrow road bridge towards Yardley Wood. *Author's collection*

The cottages by the ford in Yardley Wood Road near to where Firth Drive is now. In the 1850s Yardley Wood Road at this point was known as Wilday's Lane and later Stoney Lane. This postcard view was sent to Sunderland in 1923.

Author's collection

A horse and trap wait outside the 'Dog and Partridge' on Priory Road. Note the grand weighing machine by the entrance.

Author's collection

Yardley Wood Primary School Parents Day, 1933.   *Author's collection*

Yardley Wood Welfare Clinic, 1930. This is where children were taken for bread and butter and milk during the depression.

Author's collection

A 1920s view of Christ Church Yardley Wood, looking across the Stratford-on-Avon canal bridge.

Author's collection

Yardley Wood Bridge and Church.

Happy Valley became a popular week-end or holiday retreat in the early 1900s. It was situated near to the canal bridge on the Yardley Wood Road, known locally at this time as Stoney Lane and on the border of the Yardley and King's Norton Parishes. The attractions were boating, camping and just relaxing by the waterside enjoying the regular open air concerts. Refreshments were also available and the area, which was made to look pleasing by the local land owners attracted people from King's Heath and beyond.

Having a relaxing time at the Refreshment and Tea Rooms, Happy Valley.

Author's collection

A week end with the "Hs Hs" at Yardley Wood. The post card appears to be from Elsie and Harry Harrold who write *"How do you like the washing?"* For Birmingham folk, holidays around the early years of the century were more often spent either at Happy Valley or the Lickey Hills. A trip to the seaside would only be for the rich.   *Author's collection*

Pleasure boats aplenty on the canal at Happy Valley.   *Author's collection*

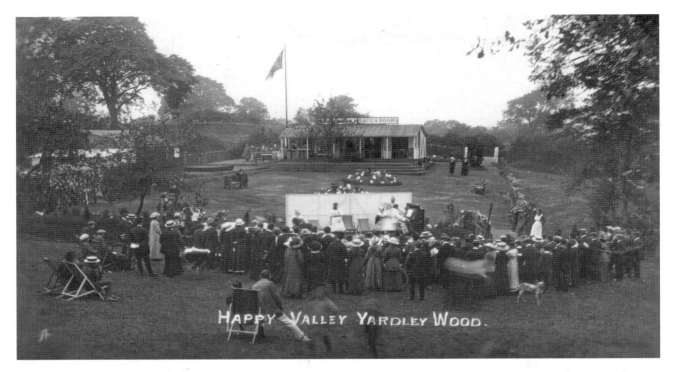

Crowds gather to see a concert performed by local players by the tea rooms at Happy Valley. They even have a piano on the stage. One would hope that the rain would keep away! On 22nd March 1935 a local newspaper reported *"Happy Valley, Application to Fair Opposed"*. An application made in Birmingham for a music licence for an Easter Fair to be held at Happy Valley (Yardley Wood) fair ground from April 18th to 23rd (excluding Sunday) was opposed by a nearby resident, who complained that the noise on such occasions was so bad that his three young children could not sleep at night.

   The magistrates granted the application, but said that if there were complaints there might be difficulty in obtaining further licences.   *Author's collection*

A family pose for the camera at Happy Valley. The young lad appears ready to use his pen knife.

Author's collection

Obviously before the call to fight for King and Country these young men, probably a sports club, relax at Happy Valley in 1914.

Author's collection

These young men with their ladies would soon have their happiness shattered by the onset of the First World War. They relax on the canal at Happy Valley during the summer of 1913.

Author's collection

An old railway wagon converted to a holiday chalet is home for these happy campers and their gramophone at Happy Valley, c1913. *Author's collection*

A concert is in full swing at Happy Valley and crowds have come from King's Heath and around to enjoy the joys of summer. *courtesy Mike Rhodes*

— NEWS ITEMS —

The following are some interesting articles from the local journals and newspapers

October 1895.

Quite a commotion was caused on the night of the 26th ult. in King's Heath by the fire on the premises of Mr. Austin, Ironmonger, High Street.

The first intimation was someone running down to the police station screaming "Fire!"

The fire, like a good many others, was caused by an oil lamp (was it made in Germany?) in the shop. Mr Austin was turning down the wick into the reservoir with result that it exploded, the flaming oil soon getting hold of the stock. Had Mr. Austin gone quietly to work instead of rushing off to the police station it would have been wiser.

Fortunately the occupants upstairs were saved—thanks to the exertions of Mr. Day (from the Brewery), Mr. Walters, and a young soldier of the Royal Warwickshire Regiment; the latter of whom found his way upstairs and fetched out the assistant, who was sweetly dreaming, quite unaware of a possible chance of being roasted alive. All this was the work of a minute or two. On Superintendent Wasley arriving, almost directly after the fire commenced, he gave invaluable directions and assistance.

While the fire was furiously raging, and had been for some time, Mr. Austin reminded Mr. Wasley that his wife was somewhere at the back of the shop! I will not repeat the exclamation which fell from Superintendent Wasley's lips! on being told this information. Without further ado, the chief of police - unable to get through the flames in the shop - went through the shop next door and got to the back, where, fortunately, he found Mrs. Austin in safe keeping. But this was not all! I might not have been alive to relate all these facts had it not been for the pluck of Mr. Wasley and one of his officers.

Here again Mr. Austin nearly made a still worse mess of it! After the fire had been raging and fortunately well got under, Mr. Austin was kind enough to inform Mr. Wasley that there was a safe in the shop which contained 40lbs. of gunpowder!!! Talk about being blown to smithereens. It is needless to say that had the fire not been got under, the explosion of the gunpowder would have wrought havoc and cost many lives.

With respect to the local fire brigade, I cannot commend them for their alacrity on this occasion. All praise is due to those whom I have mentioned and the many willing hands who assisted.

February 1899.

Many complaints, and justly so, are being made respecting the disgraceful state of some of the roads in King's Heath. Take Station Road for instance. Here one has to plough through mud and slush - well over the boot tops. If I had my way with the responsible parties, I would make them turn out and perambulate that thoroughfare for an hour or two, just to see how they liked it.

May 1899.

Messrs. James and Lister Lea & Sons were good enough to send me a catalogue, and a card to view the valuable and interesting contents of Coldbath Cottage, Billesley. The two days sale was attended by a large number of buyers from all parts of the country, while the attendance of the general public was very considerable. Among many well-known local residents at the sale were the Cartland family from The Priory.

The items for sale were of the highest quality, including old English and oriental china, old family silver and pictures. For each lot competition was very keen, especially in the case of the old china. There were certainly no bargains to be picked up as everything was knocked down at absurdly high prices.

It is somewhat surprising to think, considering its lonely situation, that Coldbath Cottage has not received the attention of "Bill Sykes". If that gentleman had only known that in this unpretentious-looking cottage there were some five hundred ounces of old family silver, he would have risked his chance of getting ten years! Such a haul would have enabled that gentleman to retire in luxury and ease for some years!.

January 1907.

A party for the poor children of King's Heath, promoted by a number of scholars of the King's Heath Adult School, took place last Saturday in the Council School. There were no less than 330 children sitting down to a substantial tea prepared by a band of about fifteen ladies, who worked hard for four hours cutting up. After tea there was an entertainment of conjuring, ventriloquism, musical instruments, and singing of popular songs, in which the children joined heartily. During the concert each child received a packet of chocolate. At the end of the party the children were told how the money had been raised and they showed their appreciation by round after round of cheering. Upon leaving each child received a bag containing an apple, an orange, and a mince pie, and in addition a woollen scarf.

March 1913.

An alarming accident, which, by what can almost be described as a miracle, was not attended by serious results, occurred on Wednesday morning, 19th Feb.

About 11 o'clock a butcher's assistant, delivering meat in Cambridge Road, King's Heath, left the horse and cart for a few moments, when the animal, from some cause or other, bolted down the road, turned into the narrow Billesley Lane, and doubled back

along Oxford Road, and at a fast pace galloped into Moseley. How it negotiated the crossing of the tram lines to Salisbury Road without collision with tram or motor car is a marvel. It continued its career down Salisbury Road, the declivity assisting its speed. It turned at Edgbaston Road and tore along by Cannon Hill Park, and, crossing Pershore Road, went up Priory Road. Here it ended its bolt by cannoning against a horse and trap outside a house at which one of Messrs. Barrow's outriders was calling for orders. Both vehicles were smashed and the runaway horse was slightly injured. The other horse escaped. No one was injured. There were some narrow escapes en route, and several people made fruitless attempts to stop the animal.

October 1914.

Patriotic Meeting at the Parish Hall. King's Heath residents have determined not to lag behind other districts in practical support to their King and Country during these trying times of the War. A crowded meeting, over which Major J. Howard Cartland, J.P., presided, was held in the Parish Hall on Wednesday, September 9th, to assist in the further local recruiting for Lord Kitchener's new army. Able speeches in support of the movement were made by the gallant chairman, Councillor Neville Chamberlain, and councillor Eldred Hallas, who one and all justified the position taken up by our country in this great struggle for freedom and right. Before the commencement of the meeting the King's Heath Brass Band paraded the local streets. The local company of the C.L.B., attired in khaki, and the Warstock troop of Scouts, were present at the meeting. Patriotic airs were rendered by the band at intervals during the evening.

10th November 1933.

On Thursday night last a serious fire completely gutted a block of workshops belonging to the Regent Woodworking Co. at the back of the premises of Messrs. Cooper.

The occupants of the adjoining shops were warned. In Mr. Pearsall's premises were a number of cattle, sheep and pigs. All except the pigs were driven into the school yard in Institute Road, the pigs being turned into the street, afterwards being found in Queensbridge Road. A telegraph pole near by was caught by the flames, the wires being brought down.

The work and repair on a slight fire which occurred at the same works recently had only just been completed.

Some sixty employees of the Company will be thrown out of work by reason of the fire.

20th May 1938.
"Air Wardens' Service Meeting at Hazelwell". The Air Wardens' Service of the Air Raid precautions scheme in the Pineapple Estate Section of King's Norton Ward, includes a large part of the extensive district of King's Heath. The section extends from Lifford Railway Station across the canal to Brandwood End, to Vicarage Road, King's Heath, and down to the Rubber Mills near Dogpool.

A meeting to recruit the wardens' service was held on Saturday night the 7th inst, at Pineapple Schools, Hazelwell. Mr. W. G. Murphy, group warden, presided. Pointing out the terrible dangers to which the people would be subjected in the event of an air raid in that district, he said that even should the danger not materialise those who joined - men and women - would derive many advantages in first-aid and other matters that would be invaluable to them.

16th March 1950.
"Sir Harry Lauder and King's Heath". The passing of Sir Harry Lauder, Scotland's greatest comedian, will be a source of sorrow to the millions whose hearts he had won by his singing.

It was in 1911 when I boarded a tram in Birmingham for King's Heath I met my friend and neighbour, Mr. Charlie Macdonald. After exchanging greetings he said *"Allow me to introduce you to my friend Mr. Harry Lauder!"* To me, it was a great surprise, though a very pleasant one. In the course of our conversation, I took the opportunity of tendering him my personal thanks for his splendid and spirited action in arousing the attention of the public to the inhuman treatment to which pit ponies were subjected. His work was ultimately crowned with success, and legislation was enacted ensuring more humane treatment of the ponies.

Sir Harry had worked in the mines for ten years and thus possessed first-hand knowledge.

On several occasions afterwards I met Sir Harry at my friend's house in All Saints Road. He was warmly attached to Mr. and Mrs. Macdonald with whom he would spend week-ends when touring in the district. His company was most delightful; he was a homely, genial and sociable man. I may also mention that the late Mr. Bob Cooper enjoyed the same privilege as myself, and on the last occasion we were together he autographed for us copies of the souvenir programme of a special concert in which he was principal artist.

The last concert at which I heard Sir Harry, he sang: *"Keep right on to the end of the road"*. The words of the song and the impressive manner in which he sang it, touched the hearts of his audience. It was more than a song-it was a sermon in music!

Sir Harry was a great artist and a fine gentleman, and though I shall not see him again, I shall always revere his memory.

Geo. Handley.

152

View of Alcester Road South c1960 looking towards King's Heath village from Alcester Lanes End with the 'Kings Arms' pub prominent lower left. An 18A bus is about to cross out of Woodthorpe Road into Taylor Road on its way to The Valley at Yardley Wood.

Birmingham Reference Library